FIGHTEY-TOWN

An Auto-Fightography

By Patrick Davis

"Life is a contact sport. You're not welcomed into this world with a pat on the cheek, but a slap on the ass. It starts when you win your first fight for oxygen and ends when you lose in the rematch. How you fare in between is determined by you."

-Martin Snow, owner, Trinity Boxing Gym

CHAPTER ONE:
FIGHTING A HOMELESS DOCTOR

"If you don't have enemies, you don't have character."
-Paul Newman

Hi, my name is Patrick Davis. I have had a crazy number of fistfights (35-40) in my life. I have an autobiographical intro coming up but I decided to just jump start this book with a fight. It's kind of like the show "Jeopardy!" We'll play a few minutes of the game first **and then** get to know the contestants!

"Discretion is the better part of valor"
-Shakespeare

"When fighting, a rich man worries about his face, a poor man worries about his coat"
-Russian proverb

FIGHTING TIP NUMERO UNO: Don't be over-confident; practically *anyone* can jack you up.

Think about it. You get a 20-ounce squirrel properly riled up and the thing can probably run up the side of a tree, dive into your face and scratch one of your eyes out. People, even small and weak-looking ones, can be DANGEROUS. If you forget that, you can lose a fight. Here's one of my most humiliating fights ever, which wasn't really a defeat, except it was in every way possible:

The year was 1999. I had gone from champ to chump in one jump. In 1998, I was in my early thirties and living The Life. I worked as little as humanly possible part-time as a housepainter, freelance writer, even a male model. I lived around beautiful Laguna Beach, renting rooms or drifting from couch to couch, or rat trap to rat trap. I had just ended a two-year relationship with a gorgeous woman who made

5

the huge mistake of trying to force me to grow up. I was really having a blast even though I was just a party-hound hobo. I had tons of girls, played beach volleyball, and went out and got drunk 6-8 nights a week. I pushed it a little close to the edge and ended up an actual bum for about a week, sleeping on the beach after I had "couch surfed" my way onto the rocks [unrelated-to-fighting life lesson: Nobody EVER feels sorry for a playboy].

I called my mom crying [some tough guy] and she flew me out to Cape Cod where I landed a good job that I got fired from, and then I decided to return to So Cal to try to make it as a screenwriter in Hollywood, yadadadada Hollywood. 1999 Hollywood was just as lovely, safe, wholesome and clean as any upscale red light district one might find in Tijuana.

Now this was before Hollywood hounded the homeless out of there with illegal private pigs. I didn't have a place lined up and arrived via bus from the airport with around 800 bucks [ok, when is the fight dude, relax I'm creating atmosphere here] and holed up in a very Bukowski-esque Roach Motel that was $100 a week. I could write several books about *that* place. I used to go to McDonalds for breakfast on Hollywood Boulevard to save money. This **was not** the type of McDonalds that you might see featured in one of their commercials.

It was a rainy winter day and the place smelled like hot garbage and 1000 wet dogs because that's where the homeless holed up in the rain, and actually every other time as well. It just smelled way worse on rainy days. You never saw three beautiful children of different races jumping into a ball pit there, that's for damn sure.

[The Hollywood Walk of Fame itself is one of the most hilarious tourist destinations in the world. You would see some blonde-haired German family get off a tour bus expecting to snap pictures of George Clooney and Charlize Theron wandering around Hollywood Boulevard dressed in Prada evening wear.

6

Instead, they would be confronted by a snake-carrying transvestite vampire runaway urinating onto the street in broad daylight. No matter how many times I saw this happen, I always got a kick out of it. It's one of those places, like Las Vegas, which is nothing like the glamorized version of what you think it's going to be.]

I had gone from suntanned, muscular beach stud to a more gray and scrawny version of myself that was always late on his rent and never had enough to eat... and in a very bad mood always. No friends, no car, no girlfriend. The closest thing I had to a friend was a guy at pizza place who looked like a Mexican version of former Lakers head coach Del Harris. He used to charge me for a personal pizza and then make it a medium, just because he knew I was starving, while nervously looking over his shoulder to see if his boss was watching. El Santo Del Harris Los Grande Pizza Upgrade!

I was hatin' life and mad at the world.

SO, back to McDonaldland, this homeless fella keeps coming up and mad-dogging me as I am trying to get into the second course of my Big Breakfast, which are the pancakes made from recycled newspaper. Dude just kept popping his head up and making a face like four feet in front of me. I finally said to him, "If you come up on me one more time, I'm going to kick your ass". Very Charles Bronson. Yes, Pat, discipline that insane person, you can do it!!! He, who like many homeless people, resembled Charles Manson, said simply:

"Do it." With considerable conviction!

I tried to back out by standing up and quietly saying, "Look, dude, things are obviously not going too well for you, you don't need more trouble-" He interrupted me-

"Not *going too well?* I AM A DOCTOR!" which, even under the circumstances, struck me as being very funny.

7

"OK, but listen-"

"No, you listen, punk. You said you were going to kick my ass, now I'd like to see you do it!" Apparently this guy had even more to be angry about than me.

FIGHTING TIP NUMBER TWO: NEVER THREATEN ANYONE, IF YOU CAN HELP IT.

FIGHTING TIP NUMBER THREE: DON'T, UNDER ANY CIRCUMSTANCES, GET INTO A *FISTFIGHT* WITH A HOMELESS INDIVIDUAL [I am guessing, however, that 99.999% of you already knew this rule].

Now, your knowledgeable and suave author of to-day would alert the ever-vigilant and Green Beret-trained security personnel at the Golden Arches. Or maybe I should have *just taken the lovely Styrofoam container containing its scrumptious yet value-priced papier-mâché bon-bons to the airy outdoor dining section*, since the gourmet treats at Mickey Ds are **designed** to be **portable,** Gentle Readers, but you already knew that. At any rate, angry, gray and broke Pat did neither of the above and stood up thinking; "All right buddy, it's your funeral."

I walked outside and I did the math. He was about average Manson-bum size, 5'5", he couldn't weigh more than 130, and I was going to pummel him. I get outside the door with him behind me and before I have stepped fully outside, he just pounces on me like a rabid housecat, filthy and SHARP fingernails tearing into my lips and cheeks and getting into my - this is going to be gross, mouth. This was a *clear* violation of The Marquis De Queensbury Rules of Polite Fisticuffs. The scoundrel would soon lose all guest privileges at the Polo Club, if I had anything to say about it.

Somehow I peel him off my face by his super-skanky coat and I start swinging him around like a rag doll. THOROUGHLY pissed, I spied a sharp, sheared-

8

off parking meter pole and was about to use it to
scrape his face completely off when I stopped in
horror. There was a fairly large crowd gathered
around. Time stood still. The rain fell. Horror
washed over me in waves as the onlookers gawped and
Charles Mansonbum, M.D., struggled feebly with his
coat pulled over his head. Achilles versus Hector
this was not. My temper dialed down a few thousand
volts and the pathos, misery and wretchedness of this
situation was not, Dear Friends, all in my head. A
Mexican guy came to the front of the crowd.

"Go ahead, heet heem, he deserve it, we all saw
heem addack joo."

Wow, I felt like quite an aristocrat there in that
moment. Classy. Any other requests, McDonalds mob?

"Do it!" He made little uppercut motions. The
crowd murmured its assent. Thumbs down indeed. I had
fought bravely; perhaps I would be given my freedom.

I released Dr. Mansonbum, who kind of gave me a
defiant look and wandered away. I looked at the
crowd for a moment, who I felt were like all giving
me the bird for at least not evening the score, cuz
my face was bleeding all over the place. I could
still smell his stench all over me, the taste of
dirty fingernails still in my mouth. Quite a way to
start the day. McDonalds breakfast, made from the
very best ingred-i-ents, "we do it all for you!"

I have never felt as wretched as I did that day
when meandering back to my Weekly Rental Tramp's
apartment, late on my rent, starving, smelling like a
hobo's sock, after getting my ass kicked by a
hundred-pound doctor bum. I was wondering if the
police were going to arrest me since I looked like a
walking horror-show; scurrying around the Walk of
Fame (in my case, Shame) with my scratched and bloody
face. Everyone was staring at me. Except for Fake
Batman, who gathered his old house drapes-cape about
him and looked pointedly away.

9

Have you ever heard the phrase "you gotta pick your battles?" It's true, you really should pick your battles.

Fighting a homeless guy was bad, but I knew I had crossed the line when I fought a handicapped guy for parking in one of *our* spaces. [badoomp-shish]

CHAPTER TWO:
"IN THIS CORNER..."

Fightey-Town, noun. Def.: A violent place in either an actual physical location or simply a violent headspace. EXAMPLE "If you keep pushing my buttons, we are going to take the train to Fightey-Town together." OR "Even now, when I see Bush on TV my stomach roils and my attitude goes straight to Fightey-Town." OR "At first blush, it looked like a tranquil 1970s Chicagoland bedroom community... but the large population of Irish made it a dangerous Fightey-Town for the children who lived there."

First of all, what kind of A-hole would write a book about all of his stupid fistfights? Good question. The short answer is: This A-hole. I have been paid (a little) to write about a lot of things, mainly humor, but I GOT TO thinking that the fights, while certainly one of the most asinine topics ever, make fairly interesting stories. Well, at least I have repeated them verbally ad nauseum, as any of my friends will tell you. Plus, I remember them all very clearly. Plus, they say a lot about me. Maybe about our world in general, but probably not. Hey, at least this tale is going to be ACTION! PACKED!

I have had about 40 fistfights or more. That's about the same amount as a family of Oakie white supremacist crank dealers. And I don't look like a fighter. Sometimes I look like one of those cologne commercial 40-year-old guys that steps off a yacht. You know, chiseled features, ascot riffling in the breeze; a gray fox with too much to lose to fight. Ha! Nothing could be farther from the truth. I am a semi-starving artist/ carpenter without a bank account who just happens to LOOK pretty good because I stay in shape... for my next fight! I kid. I play a lot of sports here in sunny Los Angeles and I am good carpenter with a surviving small business and an aspiring... well, still everything. One of my friend's ongoing jokes was that a gangbanger I beat up would show my acting headshot his boyz to organize my beatdown, and everyone would laugh - "THAT'S THE GUY WHO BEAT YOU UP?!??"

11

BUT people who fight me, I guess, think I look soft. What they don't realize is that I'm descended from the most violent people on earth... my parents [badoomp boomp shish]. Maybe there is more than a grain of truth to that. We'll go into that whole can of worms later. OK, maybe now.

I mean, I come from vi-O-lent people. My mom's side is full of fightin' Norwegian uncles who are supposedly descended from a Viking who killed a guy when he was eight years old. But that's no excuse, cuz actual Norwegians are very civilized. My dad, well, the poor guy. I think his dad beat him, and he was a corporate dude who probably half-hated his job and family. My dad was a heavy drinker who just kept it all bottled up until he unleashed some horrifying child-services-alerting-level spanking on me for, guess what, being violent! My mom wasn't all about *asking us* fifty times to shut up. It was kind of a bad scene sometimes behind closed doors of our gorgeous 4-bedroom pad in Suburban Chicago with a bitchin' lawn and full court hoops. Glen Ellyn to be exact.

And, Jesus Christ, our town itself was full of violent and horrible little rich children. I was also completely unsupervised for the majority of my childhood! [I have to tell you, though, it was fun] AND sometimes the PARENTS made us fight each other [go outside and settle it man to man and shake hands afterwards]. It was always like 20 below zero. I remember watching "Lord of the Flies" with my little sister. It's a movie [and a book, I remember reading it after punching someone out at the library] about how these little English rich kids get marooned on an island and start murdering each other. I said to my sister, "Annie, that reminds me of our childhood," she looked at me and said, "I don't remember any fuckin' palm trees."

But I live in Southern California, where most white people, especially blond-haired, blue-eyed white people are too sensible, according to my black friends, and have too much to lose to fight. And

12

there are also a lot of pussies here compared to where I come from. Where was I going with this?

When I happened upon the idea to write about all my fights, I came up with the following chapters as we in the 'biz' call them. Feel free to skip around. They are in no particular order. They are a bunch of fistfights, not like they lead up to anything such as growth or knowledge, unless you consider knowing how to kick somebody's ass a valuable thing. I can assure you that it isn't. I have never earned a penny or impressed a girl with any of these damn fights. I got stabbed and nearly died after one fistfight. I never got into another fight again... until eight weeks later with thousands of stitches still in me. OK, not every *single* chapter is the detailing of an actual fistfight. Some of the later chapters get into areas closely related to the fights. Now that I am up on the old psychologist's couch for a second, before I slug someone, let's revisit my past to highlight some child rearing factors that may have helped form my predisposition to punching more people out than Naomi Campbell:

CHILDHOOD
[1966-PRESENT]

Mary Lane was my big sister Kim's friend who was hilarious and got me high when I was like twelve. She called me Vi-Bri. Vi being violent, Bri being Brian, my middle name, which I was known by. I was always punching something or thinking about it. My parents got me a punching bag AND I BROKE IT. I actually broke the steel pin on a speed bag. My dad bought my boxing gloves when I was about seven or so and knelt down to show me a couple moves. As soon as he got down there I sucker-punched the shit out of him HARD and he just got up and walked away. He just never brought it up again.

UNBALANCED PORTRAIT?

I guess since I'm on the subject, you would think that I was completely obsessed with fighting from birth to present. NOT really. The periods in my life where I had actual fistfights were from ages 6-11, 18-22, then maybe 27 thru 43. So I didn't really fight anyone as a baby or a high-schooler. I don't think that ever was my identity anyway, like, tough guy. OK, maybe for about three years when I lived in Venice (I will get into the pointlessness of that later). In my high school, I was voted the Funniest Guy. As a kid, I was obsessed with everything from dinosaurs to aircraft to scary books and movies, to writing. I played football, wrestled and swam. But I was a very ugly and skinny kid, not a jock really. But there were THINGS.

I mean, when I think about the fights I backed out of or "pussed out" of they bring me an almost physical sense of shame. Even if it was when I was ten years old, I am ashamed of it to this day. I would lay awake many nights fantasizing about how I was going to murder my bullies at school. That's major... If you can walk away from a fight with a mentally healthy attitude, then you are more likely to become successful in life [which I am not] and not be known for pointless street scraps. At forty-four, I am a very good carpenter with talents in some artistic fields that have brought me a tiny bit of recognition. I don't know, this autobiographical shit is getting very depressing. To pick up my spirits, I am going to regale you with a tale that may have begun my actual adult road to Fightey-Town!

Author's note: As a child, I knew that when I watched "The Incredible Hulk", that Bill Bixby became a giant green Lou Ferrigno *exactly twice* in *every* episode. There isn't a fight in every chapter here, just the majority of them. This analogy isn't going where I thought it was, but if the Hulk transformation didn't happen twice, I would be very disappointed. I don't want you to be disappointed.

Suffice to say, there are PLENTY of fights in Fightey-Town, don't worry, an embarrassment of stitches, if you will.

CHAPTER THREE:
The Car Wash Fight

"The art of war is simple enough. Find out where your enemy is. Get at him as soon as you can. Strike him as hard as you can, and keep moving on."
-*Ulysses S. Grant*

"Some of the work gets kinda hard -
This ain't no place to be, if you wanna be a star."
-*"Car Wash", Rose Royce*

"As Goliath approached, David put a rock into his sling,"
-*Old Testament, or was it "Hoosiers."*

At age 19, I had misspent one year at Arizona State University. I obtained a scholarship based on high SAT scores. But my parents refused to pay my tuition after I squandered the scholarship with a putrid 0.5 GPA my first semester.

My academic fall from grace was not entirely my fault. They had thirteen different beers on tap at the ASU library and you could obtain a master's degree in something called "Bikini Contest."

I had to move home for the summer, where I lived in shame with my girlfriend's parents after getting booted by my mom. Earlier that summer, I had actually worked 7 days at McDonalds, the breakfast shift, starting at like 5am, after filling out an application as a joke. The last three days I cried on my way to work [some tough guy] and spent my afternoons looking for another job. Liz Morton was my girlfriend at the time. She was the greatest girlfriend in history. She had a little sister who was only three or so and one time her mom told her that she was washing my McDonalds uniform. Then the kid squealed in delight, "MMMMM MCDONALDS!" and went running over to the hamper and stuck her nose into my skanky brick-red Mickey Ds shirt and recoiled in horror, "eeeeeeeeeeeeeeeewwwww!!!" That was pretty

17

funny. [Sorry, this book is not an infomercial for The Golden Arches. Their "tender vittles" will not appear again for a long time.]

Then I landed a "dream job" at the car wash. It was a very sought-after gig because you would spend 11 hours a day in the hot, humid suburban Chicago sun wiping cars down, but you would actually knock down like forty in wages and sixty in tips. And to think my shmuck buddies were wasting their time in college!

There was some kind of asshole hierarchy there that I paid no attention to. We had little squirt bottles that were filled with pink Windex. One day, this fat smartass kid squirts my shirt full of that liquid for no reason whatsoever. So I squirted him back. His 6'8" friend, Richie, who also worked there, says, "You're not going to do that again." I told him to bite me and he said, "If you do it again I'll kick your ass!" I just laughed a mocking and derisive laugh. What the hell was he talking about? Was this guy the smartass' girlfriend? C'mon man. We're talking Windex here bro...

"You and ME, after work, we're fighting."

Damn. The giant not only said it, but the statement had the aura of finality. I was 6'1" but only weighed in at about 155. On the plus side, I had started an actual boxing career in a Chicago gym with a deaf former heavyweight coach, Bob Beals. Bob always began optional sparring sessions with: "OO want to Bowchx?" I used to shadow box in Liz's bedroom with foam karate gloves to the song "Take On Me" by Ah-ha (you just can't make this shit up). Anyhow, I looked reeeeaaallly far from tough. Like I said, I was painfully thin and ALSO wore horn-rimmed glasses a la Al Franken. I looked like a total fag. I don't think there was any money on me if the crew was doing any wagering. Vegas had the fight OFF THE BOARD.

That challenge was issued at around 2pm and work ended at 5pm or so. Obviously, it's a cliché but that was the longest three hours of my life. How in the wide world of sports did this happen!? A guy squirts me with Windex and thirty seconds later I gotta fight some monster? Three months ago I was playing volleyball with gorgeous coeds in the Arizona sunshine. Now I am fighting an angry ogre to save face in my career as car wash attendant. Grades are important, kids.

In retrospect, I figure it was a set-up from this one dude, John, a chubby jerkoff with a curly perm who totally hated me and was kind of the kingpin there. Over the years, my inattention to pecking orders and hierarchies has gotten me into a great deal of trouble. John even made the other guys not laugh at my jokes at lunch... is this thing on?

Right now, I want to find him and kick HIS ass, see how sick I am? [Even when I edit and reread, the thought flits through; "Where is that fat fuck?"]

Oh God, what was I going to do? The big doofus, Richie I think, just kept on leering and clowning me, saying crap like, "this is going to be fuuu-uu-nnn." Every time he passed me in our little line to get into the cars and drive them into the driveway to wipe them off, he had an intimidating comment or stare for me. The smartass who originally squirted me was chiming in as well. Everyone was treating me like a condemned man. This was taking all the fun out of working at that car wash, which wasn't all that fun to begin with.

It was very sick. Guy's 6' 8" and 210 and he has not only picked a fight with a much smaller man, but he was also already icing down the champagne for his victory party. I was thinking about trying to MacGyver my way out of the ass-whipping by making peace, but it didn't seem possible. Damn. The time crawl-l-led by 'til closing. I felt sick to my stomach but I had to pretend that I was looking forward to the fight as well.

Well, at 5pm, there was the big dummy standing there in the parking lot, waiting for me. He was

19

sort of warming up there and shaking it out, while laughing it up with his boys around him. Knowing I had pretty wimpy little wrists, I started binding my hand, boxing-wrap style, with the fruity little pink and white wife beater that I wore to work that day. It went perfectly with my horn-rim glasses. A great look for working at a car wash or starring in a Flock of Seagulls music video. My fright level was as high as it had ever been in my life. But you know what? That gives you some extra energy, if you catch my drift. My body was vibrating and screaming with terror.

I took off the glasses, so Richie was just a big tower of fuzz cuz my prescription is -6.0, and Mr. Magoo sees better than that. I walked quickly and purposefully toward him for I guess what he believed was going to be the pre-fight weigh-in, stare down, rules announcement and photo op.

I remember his confidence was just overflowing. He said, in his very annoying and nasally voice that sounded like a goose honking,

"You take the first punch and I'll finish the--" I wonder what he would have said next. Maybe "hamburger", or perhaps "Orange Julius."

Maybe. But we will never know for sure, Gentle Reader, if that next word was going to be "fight." I heard the first part of his speech and that was pretty much all the green light I needed.

The big bully dorkus never got the last word out cuz he was interrupted by just a beautiful, looping, Chuck Liddell-style, overhand right that hit him right on the temple. A sweet spot hit, not a glancing blow, THUD, oh he got alla that one. My entire body pin-wheeled into the punch, which I brought up from like a Texas border town so far south that its residents speak both English and Spanish.

He kind of shuddered and shook and bent over halfway. I took the opportunity to lay about eleven or twelve of the same punch in the same spot. It was

20

very much like those Greenpeace films when the baby harp seal gets clubbed to death. This fight was getting a lot more fun in a hurry. Curiously, he never went down all the way. He just kind of bumbled around in a circle getting beat like Neal Peart's rototoms in an extended "Tom Sawyer" concert encore. I was high on anger, fear and adrenaline. I finally stopped to catch my breath and the fight was declared over by the Illinois State Street Carwash Beef Commission. Corner stoppage, 1:18 of the first round. His boys assisted him as he staggered away, looking like he was just pulled from a bloody car wreck, when a scant hundred seconds ago he had been planning a slap-down of a harmless four-eyes nerd. [Richie, you might want to check out "Fighting Tip Numero Uno"]

I wonder if Richie had the fun he had been predicting earlier that afternoon. Was this the kind of party he had RSVP'd for?

He did not return to work for several days after the fight. Maybe he got mono. When he did return, he wore a pair of large sunglasses, like the kind Liza Minelli wears. However, one could still see a giant green and purple mushroom on the side of his big stupid head, Gentle Reader, a head that was about the size of a piano bench.

I also, seemingly overnight, got a whole lot funnier!

Moral of the story: Why fuck with people?

FIGHTING TIP NUMBER QUATRO: Don't let some asshole [like Mr. Smartass] get you into a jackpot* you have nothing to gain from. [Except a world-class beatdown by an underweight and mouthy four-eyes]

*I got that word "jackpot" from "No Country For Old Men." It is a perfect description for all the bells, whistles, commotion, and confusion of a big fight or problem. Except the particular jackpot in question is 100% bad.

21

CHAPTER FOUR:
JERRY BLAINE
BIG MOUTH STRIKES AGAIN

Sweetness, sweetness, I was only joking when I said I'd like to smash every tooth in your head

- "Big Mouth Strikes Again" by- The Smiths

Jerry is jerk [guitar riff]
Got gum on his shirt [guitar riff]
Tried to get off with his hands
And got it all over his paaaa-aaants

- "The Jerry Song" by Dan Wentz

Jerry Blaine was not a popular child. He was ver-r-y annoying. He made dumb jokes, had an irritating laugh, and if you tried to fight him he would run away and taunt you from a distance. In fifth grade, in our lovely suburban bedroom community, Jerry was having a very difficult time making friends. This was made obvious by the fact that Jerry had to be let out of school 10 minutes early by the teachers so he could run home to avoid getting his ass kicked by *the posse assembled after school*. What kind of animals were we?! What would happen if we caught him? Were we going to tear him limb from limb like a pack of hyenas or eat his flesh like piranhas?! Was some kid going to smash his head in with a rock like a caveman?! Egad.

And What The Hell were the teachers doing letting Jerry out of class early instead of trying to stop the bloodshed and violence? How about a little effort, like maybe *talking some children out of murdering* another 11-year old? I told you my neighborhood was weird, sick and violent.

Anyway, I lived about a block and a half from Jerry, so on my journeys home from school I enjoyed the company of some sadistic and horrible children

23

running alongside me in a fruitless pursuit of Jerry with his teacher-sanctioned insurmountable head start. I don't remember wearing a ski mask covered in frozen snot and nobody was wearing a snowsuit, so it had to be either May or September.

That particular day we missed Jerry, so we just milled around in front of his house for a few moments like a mob intent on burning Frankenstein or something and then peaceably dispersed. I mean, there was always tomorrow. Dare to dream. I went home to an empty house.

I remember kicking it on a brown leather loveseat, eating an after school bowl of Quisp, my reward for enduring another insufferable day of grade school and hunting Jerry down like an animal when the phone rings.

"Hello, Patrick?" An adult voice… this meant I was in some kind of trouble, as usual.

"Speaking"

"Patrick, this is Clark Blaine, Jerry would like to fight you."

"Really?" I was surprised both that Jerry wanted to fight and that Clark, Jerry's weirdo dad, was matchmaking the brawl.

Clark Blaine was a professional artist who drew pictures on the back of cereal boxes and shit. I had to admit he was the coolest show-and-tell guest ever. Jerry was once even the model for a drawing of a kid playing with the "toy inside!" on the back of a box of Frosted Flakes, the lucky bastard. It did nada for Jerry's street cred, however.

Clark kind of looked a little bit like a not-as-fat or hideous version of Rush Limbaugh with a full head of hair, one of those noses that always looks like it is sniffing in disgust, and bushy eyebrows. He also had this kind of irritating, measured, stentorian voice. Jerry's mom was very nervous and

24

pale, like woman in a Tennessee Williams play, and she hated my guts. So, apparently, did Clark. Being neighbors and of the same age, Jerry and I had tried a friendship, but it didn't take, despite Jerry's insanely awesome stash of state-of-the-art toys.

"Patrick, did you hear me? Jerry would like to fight you."

"Are you serious? Where? When?"

"In our back yard, right now." The stress had caused Jerry to lose his damn mind, apparently. Although I was about the size of a starving tomcat, I was twice as vicious.

"Sure thing, Mr. Blaine." I might have even called him Clark. My friend had a dad who had been a colonel in Vietnam and once I had learned that, I refused to call him anything but "The Colonel", even to his face. I could be obnoxious. By all accounts, I was a very obnoxious kid that many people hated.

I likely used a black rotary-dial phone to organize my hyena pack of school-age rabble. I told them to get their asses back to the Blaine house to witness my now parent-approved, *nay endorsed*, demolition of Jerry. My horrible friends were all more than happy to make the trek back. There was Brian Larson, Tim Bixler, Rob Mathews, Dan Wentz and Jim Moeller... a few others. After rounding the fellas, I just hopped over to Jerry's, using the backyard route through a shortcut in Jerry's tall hedges. And then I was standing in Jerry's aggressively stupid backyard basketball court.

Stupid because Clark, who was absurdly proud of that court and how he had engineered it, had surfaced it with GRAVEL [come to think of it, The Blaine Family Gravel Court may be the only one of its kind in the world]. He was always explaining to everyone (in his measured radio announcer's voice) ad infinitum how, because of the slope of the property and difficulty getting asphalt into his backyard, *gravel* was the only genius solution for the perfect hoops court. I guess the concrete pump hadn't been invented yet. Luckily, Clark wasn't in charge of the highway department. *Nobody* ever played hoops over there because the ball wouldn't bounce. Or it would hit a rock and go rolling down the hill. But Clark was defiant in his genius. Clark also drove a DeLorean.

Clark, like Frank Sinatra, did it his way. For good or ill. I remember how he told us in the aforementioned Oscar-winning Show and Tell appearance how he wanted to be an artist so badly when he was a kid that he had ripped out all these stitches in his arm so he could draw. That was cool, go Clark! But sometimes that stubborn individuality turned into a gravel hoops court that sucked ass, or the hare-brained idea of challenging small children to fights in gladiator matches, as if we were inmates in a California penitentiary.

Clark and Jerry approached me from the front; Jerry appeared to have been crying. They looked mildly disconcerted that I was already in the basketball court, warming up for Gravel Mania, instead of getting patted down at the front gate for weaponry. This was all strategy. It was unfriendly turf, but I was showing them that this was No Social Visit. Even at that tender age, I was as vicious and cunning as a Vietcong sniper.

I couldn't dwell on etiquette issues anyway. I had a fight to concentrate on. A weird fight, but a fight nonetheless. I wasn't really sure why I was selected to fight Jerry, but I really wanted to for some reason. Jerry and I were about the same size. Strangely, we also had the same color blue eyes and dirty blond hair. I remember this because **I hated it** when other people said we looked alike, even though I was as ugly as a plate of barf. Jerry probably outweighed me a little, as everyone did. I weighed only 80 pounds in Junior High, three years later. I remember Jerry might have actually been stronger than I was. He beat me, to my horror, at leg wrestling that year in gym class. There were no

26

weak children left in 1970s suburban Chicago; the arctic winters, unhappy alcoholic parents or wild packs of well-to-do feral children had killed them all by the second grade. I took off my shirt and Jerry did the same. I usually did this before I fought. I liked to think of myself as one of those bare-knuckle boxers I had seen in old movies.

"Patrick, you and Jerry are going to fight."

OK, sure. Clark always stated the obvious, usually two or three times.

"Jerry, are you ready?"

For God's sake Clark, can we please get on with this? I'm on a tight schedule. If you make me miss "Speed Racer", I am going to egg your DeLorean all the way back to the future after I'm done clobbering Jerry.

Jerry was *not* ready to fight but nodded. Clark stood between us like a referee in a boxing match and got the fight started with a downward Karate chop thing. For me, it was time to get this fight over with in a hurry. I felt really bizarre. Knowing Jerry to be a pussy, I just hauled off and socked Jerry in the face as hard as I could. He began to bawl. Clark sent me to a neutral corner and began to **excoriate my negative personality traits**. It is really unpleasant to hit someone in the face, but it's far worse to be on the receiving end. This was merely surviving childhood in a severely upper-middle class Crazy Town. Fightey-Town.

"THERE he IS Jerry, Mr. Big Mouth, he's sitting right there!! Mr. Big Mouth!" **Right. There.**" Yes Clark, I am right here, I can hear you too, asshole. I was sitting, right over at the edge of the gravel court, cooling off, celebrating the easy win. Now what? Do I get a Pop-tart or something? I mean, a handshake is in order, of course. BUT, Clark appeared to be *prepping* Jerry *for some kind of round two.*

27

Oh Hail no! Dude. This one's in the cooler, the Jell-O's jigglin' and the butter is getting hard. However, Mr. Blaine gave me this kind of "hang on there for a minute" stopping motion with his hand as I began to put my red flannel shirt back on. Then Clark resumed talking a bunch of third-grade smack about me. Bizarre.

I remember how weird it was that it was *an adult* totally bagging on me. He must have called me "Mr. Big Mouth" at least twenty times, and it got Jerry psyched up enough to return to the fray, with some *minor* rule changes from Clark. [I also recall vaguely thinking that there probably weren't a lot of accolades being thrown my way at the Blaine family dinner table.]

And what a **nightmare** for Clark. Everything was going horribly wrong, but he quickly improvised and spelled out which Blaine Family Backyard Beef regulations he had "forgotten to tell us". Old Clark, of course, delivered the decree with the calm deep-voiced confidence of Wilfred Brimley selling senior life insurance policies. Only now he was starting to get frantic and I could see flop sweat accumulating on his brow while his blue eyes were lurking back and forth in desperation under his unkempt eyebrows, much to my delight.

"Allright boys, there will be no punching above the neck or below the waist." He went over to Jerry, who was still crying, to demonstrate the zone he was talking about [here, not here, here, here, not here, here.] Yeah, I get it. Just say, "Don't sock Jerry in the face again," it will save us all some time. This was such *bullshit*. I had already won. *Fair and square*. In his "howse," literally, in front of his dad, who was cheating on Jerry's behalf, for crying out loud. And the "Flintstones" were starting in ten minutes. Well, despite the phony new punching sector, I had already figured out how to win again anyway.

He got the sniveling, red-faced Jerry to square up again by calling me Mr. Big Mouth about fifty more times. Within twenty seconds I was choking Jerry silly. Predictably, Clark separated us and now it was getting really pathetic, because Jerry was REALLY bawling and I started to feel horrible. I was remembering some of the *good* times with Jerry, like playing with his motorcycle-riding Evel Knievel that actually jumped stuff [Clark's job got him access to toys that weren't even out on the market yet]. Ugh, now his dorky dad was forcing me to humiliate him and then murder him. How many times and ways did he want me to beat his poor kid down? Enough was enough.

I was completely over any animosity I had towards Jerry, but I remember really wanting a piece of Clark Blaine.

Well Clark informed us that he had "forgotten" another rule: no **choking**, and I gave him a look like, "Are you dry-humping me?" And he gave me a look like, "We both know you won, you sadistic little dickhead, just work with me here for a second." Poor Clark was already going to be sleeping in the garage for a month over this one. If he pulled this stunt *today* in some overprotective wussy-ass all-white community like Laguna Beach? He'd get five years in prison and his own "Dateline" segment.

I knew what was up, but I was down with it. We had to give Jerry something to go forward with. I could discern in that moment the man's quiet desperation and love for his outcast son, and neither one of them was really that bad a guy, after all. They were just nerds. I was something of an action-junkie, but I was never an *animal*. I think Clark sensed that.

We resumed the fight with a desultory effort from Your Author, so Jerry did pretty well. We just kind of wrestled for a minute. Clark separated us and declared the fight a draw with no argument from me. I just wanted to get **the hell** out of there. Even in my insane Norman Rockwell Childhood Gone Wrong, this

29

nasty little scrape was leaving a really unsavory
taste in my mouth. Jerry could escape with his
pride; he had put up a game effort against a
psychotic foe in front of his retarded dad. My
friends weren't there anyway; Clark had turned them
away at the gate earlier. [Looking back, I kind of
admire Clark for orchestrating this bold and stupid
scenario. Clearly, as I said, it was done out of
desperation and pure love for his son.]

I told the story to my family over dinner. My
dad just laughed. Kind of irresponsible of him, if
you ask me. I have told the story to others for
years. I wonder if I left out an important detail.

...Was it me that organized the posse against
Jerry, a friendless kid? Man, cuz that would have
really been mean and not that funny.

The next fight is a fable, a tale with a moral,
and I am going to tell you the moral upfront: Don't
Fuck With People! Have I already said that? Well,
it's very important. The following fight is a
classic example of how badly things can go wrong if
you want to go around acting stupid and then back it
up with some phony tough-guy talk.

A TALE OF HORRIFYING INJURY,
THE BRIG FIGHT

"Antagonizing people to fight you is a dangerous way to make your life more interesting."
  -Patrick Davis

I used to go to this bar in Venice Beach called The Brig. It was formerly an old salty-dog bar that smelled like barf, complete with lifer alkies that got their SSI checks forwarded directly to it. But it was later converted into a really sweet hipster bar with "W-Hotel-style" decor and a rather uppity staff of good-looking bitches that acted as bartenders. It turned into a great singles bar. I ran afoul of the kind of kingpin of the uppity bitch bartenders when I asked her out and then didn't really follow up very well when my call to her went badly. She didn't laugh at my jokes in our one and only phone conversation. This happened all the time with me, but likely not to her. In dating, I have found it efficient to *lead off* with my sophomoric sense of humor, it's going to pop up sooner or later anyway. [I remember one girl looking at me in shock and awe about five dates in saying, "Oh my God, I'm sleeping with *Dennis the Menace*."]

She then got the rest of the staff to play this game where they wouldn't serve me for a half an hour when I went to get a drink, which didn't really bother me all that much, if at all. I go to bars with the buzz I already want because I can't afford to get drunk at $7 dollars a pop. Plus, I could still hit on girls while waiting, so it didn't really cause me that much pain. I also got a kick out of never letting it bother me. There is nothing like letting an insult go completely unnoted. [This diss was not a product of my fertile imagination. One of the bartenders confided in me one day that the staff was instructed not to serve me in any kind of hurry. She also told me they wouldn't tell her why.] Eventually, I became exasperated after calculating that my tips had bought them all IKEA furniture,

31

while I was sleeping on a bare mattress. So I got the manager to observe them ignoring me, which got one of them in trouble (but not fired). ENTER THEIR HERO, Cappy, which was the asswipe's name, I later found out.

I should mention that at this point in time I was pretty much all growed up. I was still 6'1", but I probably weighed a lean 200, and was referred to at the local tough hoops court as the "the white boy who scares gangsters", although I don't believe I ever carried any kind of scary demeanor. My friend said I was kind of like a lovely rich family's Golden Retriever that would bite the shit out of you for no reason.

Again, who really cares how tough the broke guy who trolls the bars is?! I guess *I cared*. At least to the degree that I believed it should have entitled me to a *little* respect. But I was often treated like a bitch, anyway. I imagine if I shaved my head and let a tattoo artist loose on me then I might have got a little more space over the years, but then I could never get a job at the Disneyland Hotel. And I like to keep my options open. Sorry, I tend to ramble.

Cappy was a kind of short and handsome Italian-looking bar back who decided to make me pay for snitching on his goddesses. He did this by shoving me when he went out to collect empty bottles. I asked him if he was out of his mind and he made a big grandstanding deal about how it was "on like Donkey Kong". Whatever, he was maybe 5' 7". The altercation was broken up. I make it a habit not to hold grudges against bar staff, why bother? This bar was six blocks from my house and I was doing pretty well with the girls there on a regular basis, AND, I was learning... pick your battles, remember? I let it go. The security guard diffused the situation, partially because I had befriended him earlier that year.

FIGHTING TIP NUMBER FIVE: If you are a person who has a violent past, present or future, get to know the security staff at the bars you frequent.

So it was over...until I went one night and Cappy was not behind the bar, but he was out in the general population playing pool. From what I learned later, Cappy had the habit of getting coked up, going around the bar, and bothering people in the bar he also worked at. When he wasn't attending Mensa meetings, that is. This can be a legitimate hobby of sorts in Los Angeles. In Chicago, this habit is likely to cause you heartache and [physical] pain. Maybe I am romanticizing Chi-town etiquette, but I just don't remember any of this stuff happening to me there. Perhaps those same sub-arctic winters and roving packs of ferocious cannibal children would have taken care of the likes of Cappy long before he had the chance to bother grown adults in social situations.

Anyway, I had also blown out my knee playing basketball and was in this giant second-hand leg brace [no health insurance] that went from my ankle to my butt so I stayed the hell away from Cappy and his coked-out capering. BUT, even though I went to the opposite side of the bar, sigh, Cappy found me. He came up to me saying something like, "Hey, this guy is really handsome, don't you think girls?" Or maybe it was something about my shirt. He was acting too friendly and yet also menacing. It occurred to me that he had now grown a big set of balls because I was now disabled. YET I had already kicked someone's ass while wearing the leg brace, a drunk who poured a drink on my head at a party, so I knew I could throw down off only one good leg. I told Cappy to fuck off and he did his grandstanding bit again. We stepped outside and he proceeded to taunt me, a guy with a bum leg, from a safe distance, WHAT A PUSSY!!! I suppose it's *possible* Cappy could have become a bigger annoyance to me, I just don't see how.

Fast-forward a couple months and the leg is OK and Old Cappy and I both show up Outside the Brig again. This time I am in perfect health. He just walks by and pretends not to notice me. Hm. I believe a salutation is in order so I asked him, "How's it going… **asshole?**"

33

He does his big theatrical production and tells me his tough-guy resume, complete with a Brooklyn street-tough upbringing [!] Gee, now I'm terrified. Knowing this wussy is just going to run away again, I start taunting him bigtime. It was pretty inventive actually. There was something about there being a statue of his likeness in the PussyBitch Hall of Fame, how he talked and never fought anyone, how I couldn't hear his taunting because he needed to stand on a couple of phone books, etc. My body language at this point is also very insulting. Where he is all balled-up across the street, I am languishing in a backwards lean, laughing at him, showing him how harmless I think he is. Yet, Gentle Reader, I am actually coiled like a snake. He must have felt very safe because there were a couple police officers 50 yards away, as cops sometimes post-up outside bars at closing time. I was also standing next to the giant bouncer. By the way, although I was acting silly, my anger level was completely off the charts. He must have felt that the next thing he did was a safe move.

He balled up his fists, puffed out his chest and rapidly rolled the hell up in my face, covering the twenty yards between us in a blustering and scary-shouting rage. My friend Chip, who knows me pretty well, said he turned his head because it was like watching a waiter carrying an impossibly high stack of dishes - and he didn't want to see what happened next. The millisecond his feet planted in front of me, the snake uncoiled and a really perfect right hand rocketed into his face. I felt a horrifying crunch, like I had hit a box of cereal [I knew what this felt like because as an insane child I had actually punched boxes of Count Chocula off the countertop all the time for some reason]. I thought, in horror, that I had caved his skull in. Curtis, the gigantic security guard, snatched me around the neck and said, "You done it now, Pat, you're going to jail." I actually had this mental picture in my head of a dark and dirty maximum-security prison upper tier, with the electric doors closing. Yay, that would be my home for the next ten years for manslaughtering a little smart-ass with an eggshell-thin, non-punch-resistant skull.

My head was down and I could only see the sidewalk. Lots of little pieces of something were

34

all over the ground...I was *infinitely relieved*, I
assumed that instead of crushing Cappy's skull, that
I had knocked out some false teeth, which turned out
not to be false.

The cops came storming over and, get this, arrest
Cappy! They had been observing the whole event and
saw him attack me. I remember a silhouetted image of
Cappy's friend putting his teeth into his front
pocket as the cops stuffed him into the squad car.
That is an image you should remember if you go around
messing with people!

AFTERWARD

A short time later, Curtis and I were talking
about the event, and Curtis remarked, "Well, I guess
he learned his lesson on that one." I remember
saying that I thought that Cappy was such and idiot
he probably actually learned NOTHING! Boy, do I know
my dipshits.

Several months later, Chip and I are standing in
the parking lot of the Venice Beach Bank of America,
and who drives up, but Cappy?! I am not going to make
eye contact because there is just no point and he
rolls right up on me, stopping about five feet away
and he sticks his chest out and says angrily, "SO,
WHAT'S UP?" I just snapped.

"WHATS **UP**?! WHATS **UP**?! YOU GET A NEW DENTIST,
MAN?!" This admonition didn't make complete sense but
Cappy got the message. I wasn't ready to patch it
up, hash it out, dialog, hug it out bitch or
apologize. I was ready to blast him again right
there. I swear it's just like that sometimes...

Cappy just walked away without saying another
word.

CHAPTER SIX:
The Airplane Fight With Sandy

I mean, this is a book of fistfights and I feel sorry about including one with a girl, although I never fought back. But Sandy fought like a guy, in every way, except that after she kicked **your ass** she would threaten to call the cops or her brother, who was nice enough, but was well-known in like 4 cities as The Last Guy You Mess With. I wanted no part of big brother Mike, not even on my best day.

The year was 1994 and I hadn't thrown any punches for a damn long time. My girlfriend at the moment was the lovely Sandy, who looked very much like a young Linda Evans. Sandy worked with me at a karaoke bar, where I was the host. Sandy didn't like the job or need the money. She took the job just to keep an eye on me. One of my life's regrets is not keeping the long letter they used to fire me from that bar, which was owned by this giant Japanese conglomerate. It was a very polite, legally-sound, and thorough detailing of the downward spiral of my appreciation for karaoke, [yes, believe it or not folks, my karaoke love affair had gone sour] as if I was going to hire a team of top-flight attorneys to bring a lawsuit against them.

Sandy used to really lay into me for being such a loser and a bum, her words not mine. She kind of picked me up when I washed up on the surf of her Hawaii vacation, we fell for each other and she had me move out to her home in Rancho Santa Margarita California; a home that she owned and bought for herself *at age 24* through her Scary German-American work ethic. She had started a daycare center after working in one, and soon she was making 100 Gs a year because she worked 14-hour days all the time. I moved in to her Dream Pad and she fruitlessly tried to rehabilitate my lazy ass from day-tripping party hound to respectable OC OG, who would soon walk down the aisle, pay taxes and mortgages, watch "Ghost" on his VCR, own a leased full-size pick-up and then purchase a top-of-the-line barbecue grill with his initials engraved into it with a fancy product purchased on QVC.

None of that, Gentle Readers, ever happened.

You know, I have had maybe 35-40 fights, and there is not a shred of doubt that Sandy could have beaten a few of the **guys** I tussled with. She had an off-the-charts unbelievably great body, blonde hair and green eyes. But she was also spooky-strong and violent. I was pretty much a Battered Boyfriend for some of that time. Every time I threatened to break up with Sandy she just beat me up or tackled me as I was going out the door, telling me I had to leave all the clothes on my back cuz she had bought them for me. She had this childhood friend, Crystal, and I asked her if **she** ever fought Sandy. Her eyes widened in terror at the memory of it. She said "yes, it was over a doll" and that Sandy went through her like wet toilet paper, throwing her on the sidewalk like a candy wrapper. Sandy once socked me in the jaw with her little fist much harder than half the dudes I fought.

We were at the Bitter End of our 2 1/2 year relationship when my mom invited us to visit her in Cape Cod. You know, just fighting 40-80% of our waking hours, and all the fights were ugly. I wanted out. Sandy felt I owed her. It was like she had rescued a mutt from getting gassed and now it wanted to upgrade to new digs. The nerve.

We get on the flight and it's half-full. I was teaching P.E. at the same school where her daycare center was located and we were both spent from work *and* the round-the-clock fighting. Curiously, the sex was still awesome.

About a half-hour into the five-hour flight, I spy a group of three open seats in the back. The dialog went something like this:

"Hey, Sandy, there's three free seats back there and one of us can lay down and sleep in them. Tell ya what: You go first [always the gentleman] and sleep for two hours, and I'll come and sleep for the second two hours."

"OK, but if I'm sleeping, don't wake me up."

"*Sandy*, that's the whole point, we're splitting the naptime 50/50. I'll give you a little extra time, but I am definitely going to sleep back there, too."

"OK, Patrick, but just don't wake me up if I'm sleeping."

She wasn't getting it.

"Sandy, this is *America*, we *share* things. You get some sleep, I get some sleep… Sandy? Sandy?" She has turned her pretty head away from me. She wheels around.

"You know Patrick, this is SO typical of you."

Oh, here weeee goooo.

"What? What the fuck are you talking about?! YOU get a turn, I get a turn, why is that so bad?"

"Its just **you**, its all about **you**, you are not a gentleman, you are selfish. Totally selfish."

"If you ask me, or anyone else for that matter, you are the one being selfish. You want to hog the whole seat for yourself."

"YOU ARE A PRICK!!!"

She has screamed this. Freaking LOUDLY. People are now watching us. I am really embarrassed. I am also short of patience so I drop the H-bomb on Sandy. For some reason, the following phrase puts Sandy in the red zone every time and I know it.

"Sandy, you need to see a *psychologist*, you are acting like a **psycho**." Sandy explodes into action, grabbing my hair and slapping me in the face over and over, not like a chick, but like a hockey player, more with the heel of her hand, and they all **hurt**. The guy in the seat behind is threatening to call the Captain and bedlam ensues. I grab Sandy and shove her roughly into her seat. She picks up a plastic fork and buries it into my upper arm, breaking off all the little points. She smiles. She has won. There is nothing I can do.

Except for picking up my cup of coffee, which has now gone cold, and splashing it into Sandy 's face and saying: "Later, psycho."

I went back to the three seats to take an uneasy nap, knowing full well that Sandy might stealthily crawl back there and murder me in my sleep with another piece of weaponry fashioned from plastic cutlery, or perhaps she would just garrote me with the plastic tubing from the drop-down oxygen mask.

I was back there for a while and eventually thought I needed to patch things up with Sandy before we landed. I returned to the seat to see a VERY disturbing sight: Sandy was so mad that she hadn't moved a muscle for like two hours. She had just sat there, motionless, like a mental patient, with the dried Sanka all over her, tripping with supernatural anger. I tried to say something, but she was almost catatonic. You have to realize how weird this is. Sandy is drop-dead gorgeous, and not a quitter. Any normal chick would have ditched me way before any of this could have happened.

"Sandy? You O.K.? You alive?"

No response.

OK, I was going to see if she was serious.

40

"C'mon Sandy... I know you are in there... Saaaaaaaandy? Are you hungry? You have been sitting like that for awhile... you want a peanut?"

I got a peanut out of the little package they give you and waved it in front of her nose. She didn't move at all. I kept waving it around and, don't ask me why, I stuck it up in her nostril.

She broke character and looked at me like I had lost my mind. She sticks her finger in there to get it out, but get this, shoves it in a *little further* with her fingernail. Now she can't get it out. Sandy starts crying. It's all too much. The worst loser boyfriend ever is going to leave her. He doesn't even realize she is trying to save his life. He has thrown coffee on her and now has gotten a Mr.Salty lodged, perhaps permanently, in her sinus cavity.

She is really tripping and crying now. I go to get a stewardess to help her but you know, being an asshole, I couldn't resist saying it:

"Excuse me, miss, do you think you could go help my girlfriend in 31C? I believe she has a peanut stuck in her nose."

"What?"

"You heard me."

HAPPY ENDING [spoiler alert]
The peanut came out and Sandy is happily married to a non-loser with winner children.

CHAPTER SEVEN:
ERSKINE

"A soldier will fight long and hard for a bit of colored ribbon." -Napoleon Bonaparte

AUNTIE: We want you to kill someone.
MAD MAX: Who's the bunny?
- *"Mad Max, Beyond Thunderdome"*

Some of the best days of my life were summers spent at the Glen Ayre Swim and Tennis Club located in Carol Stream, Illinois.

From my age 0-10 or so, the Davis family went to the Sunset Pool in the summertime, a surprisingly ghetto and crappy pool for our very upper-middle class community. Even on cloudy summer days, the three pools, Adult, Medium and Baby [which was half water and half urine] teemed with the area youth like a watering hole in Calcutta, India. I'm not exaggerating. Friends belonged to Glen Ayre, which my buddy Brad Fowlkes dubbed, "Glen Ayrian." The difference between these clubs was night and day, 2010 Ferrari vs. 1974 Ford Mustang II.

Glen Ayre's big pool never had more than a couple dozen kids swimming around. The club featured sumptuous luxuries: A high dive *without a line* of 133 shivering urchins, a huge playfield, an awesome snack bar and grill, tennis courts, and even a damn trampoline! Were there babes there? You are *killing me, Larry.* Even if a hot girl wasn't a member, she somehow found her way around the "guests only" policy, like hot girls have maneuvered since the dawn of time. My sisters and I successfully petitioned our parents to join and, for the rest of our childhood, our summers were blissful. Glen Ayre truly rocked.

We kids spent every second of every day there until the bitter winds of September brought an end to summer fun and hailed the beginning of All Things Arctic; the appalling Chicago winter; complete with bad report cards, hundred mile walks to school, groundings, and temperatures that had actually gone down to -89 degrees with wind chill.

My first summer, I met this set of twins. I don't remember their names. They were good-looking in a Leif Garret/ Scott Baio kind of way. Handsome little Italian kids with the awesome feathered hair of the era. They probably had a 55-gallon drum of Agree on tap at their house.

The lads approached me one day with a proposition as I was waiting out the mythical 45 minutes before I swam. I had likely just scoffed the sublime Glen Ayre Snack Bar grilled cheese under a decorative umbrella in an uncrowded eating area. Was it slapped together by a balding female longshoreman on winter break from our horrible school cafeteria? Hardly. A hard-bodied off-duty lifeguard named Christine, who manned the grill wearing her red, white and blue bikini top and cut-offs, lovingly handcrafted my *Frommage En Croute*. This get-up really accentuated her great legs, perfect breasts and smooth brown stomach. Not that I noticed, or remembered thirty years later. I washed the sandwich down with a Suicide, which is root beer, orange soda and red Hawaiian Punch mixed up in the same cup, as I have always been something of a foodie.

"Hey, Davis, we hear you're a pretty good fighter."

"Where did you guys hear that?" I hadn't been in any scraps at Glen Ayre, and I didn't like anything about these two, although my peacock feathers spread a bit at the mention of my skirmishing renown.

"I dunno, *around,* point is, do you wanna fight Erskine?"

"What the *fuck is an Erskine?"* Erskine didn't sound like a kid's *name;* it sounded like an expensive fur coat or maybe a vicious badger of the Russian tundra.

"Some kid, he just wants to fight you. You **chicken?** He's not even in your grade. He's in third and you are in fourth, it should be easy." The sunlight gleamed in one of the twins' coiffures, a gentle breeze riffled through his brother's. Their angelic faces betrayed no ill intent. They acted like setting up pool fights between two school-age strangers was the most natural and normal thing in the world. Summertime fun.

Hmm. An easy fight against some arbitrarily pugnacious kid with the unlikely name of Erskine... *intriguing.* I scratched an imaginary beard that has never come in to this day. I *did*, admittedly, enjoy the occasional spirited dust-up. Scrapes and bloody noses were no big deal to me. I considered myself a man of action, yet. Yet, also a man of reason. To this point in my life, there had to be *grounds for a fight,* and usually damn good ones.

"I don't even know who the hell he is. Why does he want to fight me?"

"He just DOES, I mean, if you don't want to..." [eyes roll, bored and imperious sighs abound]

Their teen idol looks and annoying demeanor made my decision for me. I really just wanted to punch *them* out because they were a couple of condescending, pretty-boy wussies. I would just have to settle for their buddy, *Erskine*, who *had to be a* soft little bitch to be rolling with the likes of these two.

"Sure, I'll fight him. What the fuck." [I swore so much as a kid, Robbie Mathews' mom periodically banned me from their house and I was NEVER allowed to vacation with them] What the hell. A third-grader. His funeral.

But who the hell was Erskine? Why were these creepy little perverts setting up a fight with the two of us? Did they have a beef with me? Were they just bored? I couldn't have possibly had a problem with this mysterious kid, who I later learned went to Ben Franklin Elementary, while I attended Hawthorne. Strange. Another reason that I hadn't met him was that he was *a guest* that day and not a member. Reading this back, this fight reeks of a rigged set-up. I'm sure they invited Erskine to the pool that day for the express purpose of kicking my ass. I probably had made a derogatory comment about their hair at some point. Or maybe they were just like young Romans bored to deviant behavior by luxury. They had grown weary of the sublime and decadent pleasures of our well-appointed Swim and Tennis Club and needed the diversion of some gladiator games... maybe after a gay locker room orgy or subsequent to vomiting up their ice cream sandwiches just so they could eat a Push-up...I mean, they *were* of Italian descent.

They went off to summon *The Erskine* and promote the fight.

The first time I laid eyes on the kid I was to battle was about thirty seconds before it went down. I might not have made the decision so quickly and carelessly if I had seen the kid before. He was about my height but buffed in that weird way really strong children can be. He had like a six pack and chest muscles, and red hair. Red hair was always a bad sign. I didn't develop chest muscles until I was 34. He looked very weird. He had a very pugilistic-looking upturned nose and these spooky red-brown eyes that kind of jiggled in their sockets psychotically. Egads, this was no schoolboy, they had summoned The Kraken from the depths of Hades!

He wore a black Speedo and I wore a blue one. Required gladiator attire for Chi-town poolside beefs set up by the Leif Baio Twins Summertime Fight Management Company.

We met and shook hands or whatever right outside the snack bar. There was no grandstanding or mad-dogging from Erskine. He was all business and likely a professional. I wonder now what currency *this assassin* was paid in. Perhaps a couple packs of football cards with the little pink slice of cardboard gum inside, or maybe a basket of fries. Most likely it was just the respite from the horrors of Sunset Pool for a day and the promise of another one.

I think there were about four or five kids watching. I think it was a cloudy day so there weren't many people around. It being 1979, there were no parents anywhere, per usual. A couple real cute girls were there though, including the ridiculously beautiful Ellen Berry, which made what happened next so much worse.

At the beginning of the fight, Erskine [I later found out this kid's name was *Todd* Erskine and he used that buff body to become a good gymnast in high school] bobbed, weaved and then just unloaded a very mean right to my jaw. KLOK! All the fight went straight out of me. It was the hardest I had ever been hit in my life. I started crying [some tough guy] and the twins intervened and called the fight. It's the only fight I can recall where I didn't even fight back. I got TKO'd nine seconds into the first round!

Those little bitchass twins just gathered up their togas, threw a laurel crown on Erskine and had some insincere commiserating words for me. They wandered off to have sex with a couple slave girls, blow-dry their hair or supervise a crucifixion. *The gladiator games were a BORE today, Leifus. We imported that savage Erskinus all the way from Germania to the baths for NOTHING! Make sure to feed Davis to the lampreys slowly. He wasn't worth the two sesterces we paid for him... gladiator, my ass! Indeed, Baiocus, now where is that damned ice cream truck driver? If that Silesian pirate is late again with our Strawberry Shortcake bars, I shall have him flogged! Oh, don't forget to pay that animal his thirty pieces of Bubble Yum, I hear it's made with spider eggs anyway.*

47

I had a bad memory that would last a lifetime for getting taken out by a kid that was a year younger than me in front of chicks. I never saw him again.

Even though it was about a hundred years ago, I hate thinking about this fight to this day. Yet it was not without its lessons:

FIGHTING TIP NUMBER SIX: Be very leery of set-up fights.

FIGHTING TIP NUMBER SEVEN: Don't fight people you don't know for no reason.

CHAPTER EIGHT:
JAIL FIGHT

"The best victory is when the opponent surrenders of its own accord before there are any actual hostilities. It is best to win without fighting."
-Sun Tzu

THIS tale has plenty of interesting characters and wondrous insights into the human condition, jail and fights. You know, all of those things that everyone enjoys enjoying vicariously. The real thing? Not so much, that's for damnnnnnn sure.

I wound up in OC jail with a sentence of 90 days for my failed Jewel Heist. See appendix under "Jewel Heist". OK, there is no appendix in this book. You will have to wait for the sequel, "Dumbass-ville".

I remember clearly how scared I was when the doors of the 80-man tank closed behind me. The guards have a very limited jargon they use when addressing the guests, boiled down to, "Get the fuck in there, no in THERE, dumbass" and "shut the fuck up." In booking, there was actually a pretty funny guard that gathered the other guards around and was like, "Hey, look at Surfer Joe here, Hey Surfer Joe, you're not supposed to be in jail, you are supposed to be at the Wedge, shooting the curl, hanging out with the babes!" His good will, humor and cheer were the exception and certainly not the rule for the staff, which had a pretty awful and dangerous job, to be fair. It was, however, pretty clear I didn't look like anyone else there. Great.

After I was told to get the fuck in there, no THERE and to shut the fuck up, my wondrous experience in the maximum security level of the Orange County Jail, Santa Ana branch, began.

I was issued the de rigueur outfit of the season, orange jump suit, and soon learned All Was Not Well in our lovely cage. Timmy was kind of a one-man welcome wagon assigned to me to give me the rules and regs, the dos and don'ts, the Goofuses and Gallants of lock-up. He actually did quite a nice job. Timmy was sporting a mean shiner from the last night's schedule of activities. Which was, oh nothing, a race riot.

"Ok, you ever been to jail before? I didn't think so. It's cool, we need a good-sized wood right now, cuz we just had a wreck with the beaners and the shit went down."

He saw the quizzical look on my face and tried to translate what he said into plain English.

"OK, I'm a wood, you are a wood. Wood means you are WHITE. OK, we are in a 80-man tank and the guards are never down here but when you see one you yell, "MAN WALKING" and if you are supposed to shut up, someone will yell, "RADIO THAT SHIT."

Huh? My intrepid native guide shrugged as if he knew that certain subtleties, customs, jargon and morays would simply have to be absorbed via *osmosis*. He suddenly brightened.

"Man, the guys are going to be happy to see a big wood." Timmy led me through a labyrinth that led to an 80-man barracks. It didn't have that April-fresh smell. Everyone kind of scowled at me as I was led to my bunk, which was metal painted an ugly brown color with a stinky little wrestling mat-type "mattress" on it.

As far as atmosphere goes, think "Cool Hand Luke". It was poorly lit and crowded. We were in the basement of sorts and there were no windows and pretty much nobody to scream for help to. I mean, I'm not fussy, but there was nothing charming or cheerful about the place at all. It had that odd smell that all jails have; the enticing aroma of stale air, bad breath, fear, Pine Sol and "who cut the cheese?"

Timmy lowered his voice. As a newcomer, my assigned bunk was in enemy territory. Jesus, I was scared. But I figured if some of these little guys were surviving, I should be OK. I mean I was in absolutely phenomenal shape, literally, the best shape of my life. But I also felt very awkward, looking tan and healthy while everyone else, at least the white guys, was the color of old white tube socks that had been washed gray.

"OK, the Chicanes, that's the Mexicans, outnumber us in here like two-to-one. They started to tax us. They wanted the wood car to pay them like a can of coffee every week and our shot-caller told their shot-caller to fuck off and then the shit went down in here, and there is like a temporary truce that nobody thinks is going to last... car, you know? Your car is your race; you are in the wood car. The Chicane car is Mexicans that were born here, the Border Brothers are illegal Mexicans and they weren't in on the fight, they stayed, ya know, neutral or whatever. The Toads are the blacks and they don't really matter cuz there's like only two of them." Wow, lotsa information.

"Hey, Timmy, you fuckin lop, shower wino!!" Someone called out. Timmy gave a sheepish smile. "Shower wino" was a common insult and or salutation. A wino is the lowest form of life in jail terminology. It means you are a bum whose standard of living gets upgraded by 3 hots and a cot.

"You need a welfare kit cuz you ain't got store yet, you got any money on your books? Never mind... I'll get you some shower shoes. If you are caught off your bunk without your shower shoes, you get a warning, if you do it again, you get taxed. If you slam the phones once, you get a warning, if you do it twice, you get taxed." I had no idea what shower shoes or slamming the phones was... or what "getting taxed" meant, but I would find out and not do it, that was for damn sure.

51

["Getting Taxed" is a disciplinary measure where three members of your **own car** stand in a circle around you and punch you as hard as they can anywhere not in the face or balls for about thirty seconds. Toward the end of my sentence, I was asked to participate in this ghastly ritual as a "tax-er" and begged off claiming a hand injury. God knows when that horrid memory of "taxing" some poor loser could pop up; during my baby's first steps, sex, viewing a rainbow, etc.]

"Uh, I'm going to introduce you to the other woods."

Timmy introduced me around to the white car. He was kind of proud like he had brought home a new puppy. These guys were really tense and glad to see another "good-sized wood". Despite the terror of my new situation, I was still kind of internally laughing at this weird homo-erotic terminology and the absurdity of being referred to by other grown men as a "good-sized wood". Ew.

I had done it again, fucked up my wet dream life of sun and fun and wound up in a gladiator race war in the span of twenty-four hours.

What a fool, I had thought that just *being incarcerated*; the shame and inconvenience of being behind bars, having a deputy feel your nuts with rubber gloves, crapping into a toilet in full view of others, eating baloney that would make a rat barf [*not to mention* being away from girls, drink and sunshine], would be *sufficient* punishment in the eyes of ones' peers. Yet now I was also being co-opted forcibly as a "good-sized wood" into some half-assed race war while my own beliefs were **strictly** of the Rainbow Coalition variety.

I wasn't, however, asked *my* opinion on racial equality and I didn't think it wise to offer it.

Well, I thought huffily, if I survived these numerous and varied dangerous and politically

52

incorrect humiliations, my congressman was going to get quite an earful. Quite. An. Earful.

It would seem, to the outside observer, that the county had little love in its heart for me, and cared not at all for my personal safety. This turns out to be true in many jails, especially the bigger ones. If you break your leg, as inmates say, you are lucky to get a kickstand.

The food was almost comically bad. But the county also *sells* inmates snacks and various sundries like combs and the aforementioned shower shows [crap-tastic 39-cent flip-flops sold for two bucks, designed to curb athletes foot]. I had "no money on my books" because I didn't tell anyone on the outside where I was; all my friends thought I was out of town. I maneuvered to eat everyone's leftovers at mealtime by strategically placing myself in chow line with the lightest eaters. It became pretty hilarious one day when I ate with three tiny Asian dudes who couldn't finish their, for once, giant breakfasts in the three minutes we were allotted to eat. To their wide-eyed amazement, I ended up doing four bowls of oatmeal like they were Kamikaze shots as time ran out. But that was all later on when I became more comfortable [and to some degree feared]. Those first days were filled with the terror, disillusion and remorse of paying to see, and then sitting through, a Hugh Grant movie.

I have really desperately needed a life coach at several stages in my life, but like Clark Blaine and Frank Sinatra, I did it my way.

Timmy introduced me to the distinguished varsity unit of the wood car. The peckerwoods. Woody Woodpeckers. The Tiger Woods. OK, nobody was ever called "Tiger Woods."

There was "Cactus Jack From Sugar Hill, never worked and never will," another guy who was really funny and if anyone laughed at one of his jokes, he would say, "Hey GUYS, isn't this GREAT, I mean, it's just the BEST." Another guy who dubbed me "Calvin

53

Klein" and our shot-caller, who was negotiating a peace treaty at the time with the Chicanes. We Woodrow Wilsons fervently hoped he was going to be successful.

Kids, obey the laws. They are the glue that holds our society together. Stay in school. Stay outta jail.

Where were the guards? Where was the supervision? Oh well. No use crying over spilt milk.

When the guards came in for head count, you were supposed to be on the bunk they had assigned to you. Right afterward, you went to the other bunk that your car assigned to you and spent the rest of your day and night there. The bunk I spent my first day was adjacent to two of the Chicanes responsible for the riot. They were tiny, I mean smaller than eighth-grade girls, but were overflowing with confidence and attitude.

Supposedly they were 'shooters' on the "outs" and feared and respected. They didn't like me **at all** and began antagonizing me from the get-go. I think by the second day they had thoroughly gotten on my last nerve. But what was a soft and sheltered white boy like me to do? Their derision went something like this:

"Hey, homie… did you fart or something? Cuz it stinks in here. Hey, homes, I'm talking to you."

"No, I didn't fart."

"Well, make sure you don't, cuz we don't like bunking with a wino that stinks."

"Yeah, you stink, homes."

Laughter.

Well, I really didn't know what to say about that.

Outwardly blank, I was ready to kill them. Literally. For one thing, I wasn't in that great a mood. I was filled with self-loathing, anger and despair. After living in terror for a couple days, I was getting the lay of the land and I wasn't as intimidated by the surroundings. If this was the jungle, I could actually be the Apex Predator of this shit hole, if I had really cared to be. Most of the guys in there were wimps, if you want to know the truth. It's not as if many of them were captain of the football or water polo team.

Another thing was, the two Chicanes might have been feared shooters on the outside but I didn't see any guns laying around there anyplace, if you catch my drift. I was pretty sure my ex-girlfriend would be able to body slam either one of them.

Plus, I had done absolutely nothing to offend anyone. I had checked my loudmouthed, funny, effervescent and opinionated personality at the cellblock door. These people didn't seem to appreciate *that I was really making an effort*. The nerve.

I was a quick study of the jailhouse rules. I WAS DETERMINED not to have any problems that would lead to injury or a longer sentence. But I had sort of snapped. I went to the leader of my car, who was this really nice guy that seemed like kind of a bearded intellectual. All jail fights have to be approved, scheduled and **then bet on**. Parliamentary procedure must be observed!

He was reading a copy of Barely Legal as I approached his bunk. He closed it and put it neatly in a plastic wrapper and asked me what was on my mind.

"You know those two Chicanes in the bunk next to mine? I want to fight them both, in the TV room, both at the same time, I mean." TV room is where you fight people; it was farthest way from the guards.

55

Everything in the TV room is either concrete or steel. As any military man will tell you, knowledge of your terrain is critical.

I had done some calculations that evening after being called a dirty wino by two guys whose bloodlines probably included rats and mice. I have to tell you, it felt good to be thinking about going on the offensive instead of worrying so much about my defense for a change. I thought about the potential fight in strategic terms.

I was big, fast and strong. Surprisingly fast, just ask Cappy. I was bench-pressing 265 at the time, whereas now I probably couldn't put up 200. If I were set in a concrete room with the two of them, I would just have to disable one of the weak and tiny SOBs quickly and then take care of the other one before his little rat claws could scratch my eyes or whatever. Neither weighed more than 120, so I thought I could smash somebody's head against concrete or metal before the other one even figured out what was going on.

The whole thing could take less than 45 seconds. It was actually going to be an easy fight. If I made the first twenty seconds so violent and horrible that it inspired fear and terror, then not only would I win the fight, but I would be able to do the rest of my time in peace. I was looking forward to it. It had been a pretty bad week and I was ready to let some shit roll down hill. And although I felt it was actually going to be a ridiculously easy fight, it had "legendary" written all over it in capital letters.

Our shot-caller looked at me with raised eyebrows. This was a highly unusual request.

"Let me get this straight, you want to fight **both** Chicanes at the same time in the TV room."

"Yeah, both of them, same time. Can you make it happen?"

56

"I'll have to get back to you on that one."

I was really hoping it was going to go down. I was in a really, uh, **weird** mood. My exposure to mistreatment, humiliation, crappy food, mistaken fart blame, terror and fear was getting to me. It was also the longest I had ever gone in my life without a beer. So I was a little edgy.

Now I had found the perfect outlets for my frustration. Two overconfident little murderers were gonna find out precisely where they stood in the old food chain. This was going to be Godzilla versus Bambi and Thumper. Skulls were gonna be cracked, arms were going to get broken... I was never more ready to fight in my whole crazy life. They thought they were biting into a big soft, white birthday cake, except the filling was going to turn out to be rattlesnakes, scorpions and black widow spiders.

I was summoned to our shot-caller's bunk later that day.

"Sorry kid, you ain't gonna fight the two Chicanes."

Damn. **It.** The air went out of my rage balloon.

"Why not?"

"We are trying to iron out a wreck here, and you fightin' two tamales would just make it worse. They probably wouldn't agree to the fight, but if they did, you can't win."

"I can take them, trust me..." It was the only thing I had been looking forward to. I hadn't even been sentenced yet, so I was facing anywhere from 90 days to a year [it was 90 days].

He looked at me for a moment. "Yeah, maybe you could, but if you win, you are going to lose. It would be just too embarrassing for their car and the

Chicanes would beat you down in the lunchroom, or you'd get shanked in the shower if you won. If you take on one bean, my man, you take on the whole burrito."

"Damn."

"Yeah, they are little turds. They started this whole shit with the coffee. I'd love to see you do it, but it ain't gonna happen." Ah, the wisdom of King Solomon, THANK GOD, or I probably would have been murdered.

"But, Davis?"

"Yeah?"

"You are definitely OK in my book. You are getting a bunk in the penthouse area now."

"Huh?"

"The fifty-yard line, top of the woodpile, you know, with us."

"Thanks, man."

"No problem, dude, just do your program, you'll be back surfing in no time."

And do you know what? I was!

CHAPTER NINE:
HERO? OR ZERO
THE SAGA OF BILLY, WARRIOR PRINCESS

"If you are going out for a fight leave your best hat at home.
-Japanese Proverb

A dozen of the UCLA Dream Team that saved my bacon, against long odds, gathered around my bed on the first day my breathing tube was removed to tell me how proud they were to have saved my particular life. The police, inexplicably, had told the staff that they had saved the life of a hero. In a life that has been painfully short of real achievement, it was a magical moment in a very horrible time. I had no idea the police held me in such high regard; I thought they had the **opposite** opinion of me. They were referring to the following chain of events:

BILLY, WARRIOR PRINCESS

"One of the most time-consuming things is to have an enemy."
~ E. B. White

Sometime in 2005, I was riding my bike down the Venice Beach Boardwalk at dusk. There is probably no better place to ride a bike. You can go to dozens of shops, bars, basketball courts, volleyball courts, restaurants, etc. and the weather is usually great, day or night.

There are certain dodgy places in Venice that are best to avoid at certain hours. One is near the corner of Rose and Speedway, where I was riding my bike one evening when I stopped to watch a curious scene in front of a bar called Venice Bistro.

One of the ubiquitous Venice local skateboard thugs was arguing vociferously with a homeless man. The thug was tall and thin, almost 6'6", and the

59

homeless guy was bespectacled and rather innocuous-looking. As their altercation escalated, the homeless guy, to bring comic relief, brought out his squeegee and said, "You can't mess with me, can't you see that I am well-armed?" The thug's thug buddies, witnessing this exchange from the bar on the outdoor drinking area, made a bunch of catcalls and laughed in derision.

Playing to the crowd, the homeless guy made some sword motions with his little squeegee to stir more laughs. The thug then brought out a very scary looking butterfly knife and advanced on the homeless man, jabbing at him. I intervened, "Hey, dude."

But then the homeless guy took off and, fast as a SWAT team, the thug's loser buddies lit off after him. SCUM apparently live for moments like these. In a matter of ten seconds, the gang had caught up with the homeless man, had thrown him to the ground and was kicking the shit out of him. Really hard. I yelled that the police were coming and they kind of dispersed. The homeless man slunk off to wherever homeless men go to heal grievous wounds, and the thugs returned to The Bistro to celebrate and then probably discuss whether The Iliad was better in the original Latin.

I think that's what angered me the most. They sat around drinking beer, laughing. The sadistic cowards acted as if they had just climbed Mount Everest. I sat on my bike watching them. I **had** to say something.

"HEY, that was pretty cool. You sure you had enough guys to take that one little dude down? You guys are **really tough!**"

They kind of all looked at me like angry cavemen and muttered vague threats about me being next. But they were satiated, their cowardly hyena bellies bloated with carrion, and I left, seething. I wasn't really in the mood to be threatened by these pieces of shit so I wanted to be sure, Gentle Reader, that at least one of them would make it onto my VIP list.

A list with precious few benefits and no expiration date, by the way.

I looked at them all, noting their faces, knowing I would run into one of them sooner or later.
It was sooner.

[I believe our country's disregard for the homeless is disgraceful and reprehensible. *Having been homeless,* I know the misery, terror and despair of the predicament all too well. To add injury to one of these unfortunates, who have no place to heal, rest or get medical treatment {many cities refuse them care} I believe to be an act of purest cowardly evil, especially when done **by a group for amusement.**]

Two days later, I go to my favorite Venice coffee shop, Abbots Habit. It's where dirty hippies chill with movie moguls and heads of state. I am standing in line and **there is one of the dudes.** There are about 30 or so locals in the place, so I decide to introduce him to the assembled crowd. I have a very loud voice… years of Julliard training, Don't Chew Know. From the diaphragm:

"LADIES AND GENTLEMEN, I'D LIKE TO INTRODUCE THIS FINE YOUNG GENTLEMEN RIGHT HERE. HE AND HIS FRIENDS LIKE TO GANG UP AND PUMMEL THE HOMELESS."

Turns out, the guy's name was Billy. Billy looked very much like a thinner version of the bully 'Nelson' from The Simspons, only older and with long hair. He usually wore jeans, boots, and a black concert t-shirt with the sleeves cut off, showing off his rather unimpressive 'guns' and bad tattoos. He probably only weighed 160, but he kind of had this tough-guy walk and sneer like he was two-hundy.

He did not *care* for his introduction *in the least.*
Oh well.

He wheeled around and got extremely red, his ugly face contorted in scary rage. He choked out his

61

threatening words to me from a distance just out of range of my right cross.

"You don't know what **the fuck** you are talking about. You can get **fucked up** for talking shit about people."

Oh boy, was he really going to make it this easy for me?

"Well, who's gonna fuck me up… you?"

"Yeah! Me!"

"Hows about right now!?"

"Yeah, right now!"

Welll alllllllllllllllllrighty then, mission accomplished. I had lured one of the villains into that old briar patch. Cue the music, "Welcome to the Jungle", and crank it up loud. This guy was going to get beat like a rented mule. Did I say I don't like to fight? Did I say that? For once, the right guy was getting it. [I often think that one poor shnook gets the ass-kicking for the last 20 dudes I have let off the hook, and sometimes the punishment doesn't fit the crime, but this guy couldn't have been a more deserving candidate.]

All of sudden, his slutty little druggie-looking girlfriend starts in, "You weren't even there, he wasn't even there, you don't know what you're talking about. Yore bout to get your ass kicked"

Shadddap bitch, I thought to myself pleasantly. I ignored her. I was sniffing the air like an animal. I was going to eat Billy's liver with fava beans and a niiiice Chianti, thupthupthup.

Kidding aside, I am actually stoked. Sometimes being good at fighting really can pay off, like it was about to. Any fight brings a lot of anxiety. If you have ever been in one, you know what I am talking about. No matter whom you are fighting, it's scary. I was a little fearful, even from dildo-juice here, but not much. There were some rapid calculations involved.

This particular type of bully was my absolute specialty at beating down, The Fake Tough Guy. As I mentioned, I am around 6'1", 205. In good times most of that is bone and muscle. I'm athletic and quick. I eat really well. Some junk food, but mostly eggs, wheat bread, steak, fish, fruit smoothies, imported beer, etc. Aside from way too many Fritos, Doritos and fast food burgers, it's a diet shared by many large athletes. I lift weights, train or play sports 4 times a week. I won the silver medal in the Chicago Boxing tournament and wrestled in high school. I have won around 35 fistfights and lost maybe two.

But to many, I wouldn't be the favorite. Cuz, gee, he looks so scaaaaary. I mean what with all the long hair, scowling and Scary Band Concert t-shirts!

My opponent is 5'10" maybe 160 and likely on The Scumbag Miracle Diet: Cheezwhiz, Fluffernutter, M&Ms, Skittles, smokey links, cigarettes, crystal meth, skunk weed, wonder bread, and just enough Sunny D to prevent scurvy. This guy's idea of a hot meal comes from a glass case at 7-11 or AM/PM. He drinks soda pop with every meal, including breakfast. Oh, but the tattoos indicate that *he can handle himself* because they will *only* tattoo hardasses at the tattoo parlor. [I mean, they do background checks to make sure that you are an internationally-known toughman before they take your $50 and ink a permanent picture of a goblin or Skeletor on your ass.] Not every guy that gets tattoos is a pussy, but have you ever seen a nature show where a certain species of harmless snake mimics the markings of the poisonous one? Well, that survivalist imitation happens **a lot more often** among the old Homo sapiens, or Homo erectus, Homo Habilis or whatever type of missing link Billy and his ilk actually are.

Also, if Billy has an exercise regimen it likely consists of riding his hog and slapping his old lady around.

I know I am going through him like a fullback exploding through that circle of paper at the homecoming game. I don't care if he has studied under Freddie Roach, Royce Gracie and the ghost of Bruce Lee. I am just too big, strong and angry for him. I am also righteous. Let's commence to jigglin!

We step outside and he says he's gotta put his breakfast in his truck and then I'm in big trouble, and suddenly this bitch emerges with:

A can. Of pepper. Spray.

He tries to squirt some on me and misses. He beats a hasty retreat. I start laughing at him.

"Hey, bitch, you got your rape whistle, too?" I allow him to run and weasel out. There will be another day. He and his biker mama drive away yelling curses and calling **me**, inexplicably, a pussy.

People in the outside seating area could not believe what they just saw. The scary biker dude breaking out a can of pepper spray after challenging a guy to a fight. Pussy Hall Of Fame. First ballot. Finally something Democrats and Republicans, Muslims and Jews, East coast and West coast rappers can agree on: this dude is a *bitch*.

You have to realize that I never attacked him. I just pointed out his hobby of beating up the homeless. HE challenged ME to fight and then busted out some pepper spray, his first of many cowardly acts.

Did I bait him? Yes. Did he deserve to have his hobby pointed out? You think so? I know so.

64

The next time I saw him he tried to pepper spray me again and the NEXT TIME after that I walk up to the coffee shop and there he is, with his back to me, in a line going out the door, with a can of pepper spray IN HIS GODDAMN HAND. What, does he now sleep with it under his pillow too?

His impregnable armor. His Excalibur if you will. Would I dare attack the noble Billy, Warrior Princess of the Homeless Beatdown Roundtable when he was fully armed with Peppercalibur? I didn't stand a chance against its spicy power. A cayenne mist of certain death. Part of me was in fear and awe of this awesome aerosol can of destruction, but another part of me wasn't really. That part of me was getting really sick of his numerous and cowardly insults to mankind, manhood and the honorable way of doing things.

Billy was under some kind of nutty and short-lived misperception that the rules of society were protecting *me* from *him*. That answer is incorrect, sir.

Anyhoo, the "No Rules"-loving Patrick noticed he had his lovely locks in a ponytail that day.

I paced back and forth quickly nervously and wondered if Our Friend Upstairs had laid out this little banquet just for me. I was very worried about how the folks on earth in the cheap seats would view my next move, but pretty sure how it would be perceived by the fans in the Great Luxury Skybox in the Clouds. That, my friends, is the question you should ask yourself when the chips are down; yet know that the answer will never be easy. I made the decision based on my desire, let's say, to stay in the good graces of my Boss.

It turned out to be pretty fun as well.

I just walked up and as he turned to squirt me, I slapped old Peppercalibur out of his hands, reached out and spun him around by his shoulder, then grabbed his hair with both hands as you would hold an axe, a golf club or a baseball bat. I then swung his head toward the ground like someone trying to win a stuffed animal at the fair with a sledgehammer. Some tough guy. I've had a harder time exterminating a resilient cockroach.

DING! Bam, his head hit the pavement. Peppercalibur skittered harmlessly away, its tangy chipotle-flavored magical powers rendered useless. I remember a kind of nerdy hipster dude surveying the series of events with a look on his face like E.T. just landed in front of him. It was pretty violent. Oh well. He appeared to still be alive after this blow so I dropped a couple rights into his face and exited the premises, saying, "Why don't you take that with you?"

Dirty hippies thought the violent scene was a drag, movie moguls saw the fight as miscast, and heads of state crossed Venice off their list of "places to retire".

Justice served.

I left. I had done my good deed for the day. Yes, Gentle Reader, your narrator had slain the dragon!

Not really, it was the beginning of this half-assed feud that landed me in jail with a $150,000 bond, but more on that later.

CHAPTER TEN:
NEAR-DEATH EXPERIENCE

Don't bother defending the honor of a woman who doesn't have any" - Patrick Davis

God, DAMN this story is filled with whatever... drama, I guess and it brings back some OF THE WORST memories ever. I'll just start at the beginning. This is a severely long story so I advise that you go get a snack* [if you know where that quote is from, 100 bonus points].

I met Ennis through his girlfriend, Claire. Claire was a semi-cute redhead chick that was a skateboarding smartass in Venice. I used to see her around and we'd chat from time to time. She was kind of a local character. I guess we were both were.

I was looking for a room to rent. My current roomie and I were at odds. My lifestyle vs. her Post-Its.

I saw an ad at the local pizza shop for a room for rent, and it turned out to be Claire's ad. She had a black boyfriend named Ennis who I met a few times but knew nothing about. He also skateboarded, smoked a lot of weed, and wore this cool black and white-checkered ska-style hat... your typical friendly neighborhood guy with no job or visible means of support.

Anyway, I moved in with Claire, a chick I barely knew, and Ennis, who was not technically a tenant, but happened to be there all the time. Tra la la, what could go wrong?

Things were good at first. Ennis and Claire were on their best behavior. We kind of hung out and chilled together and had some laughs. Aside from the fact that Ennis was always having his kind of loser skater "guests" in the house all the time, it was OK. Again, he wasn't on the lease, but in actuality he was the most present and annoying "roommate". My tolerance was sky-high, though. It was like $550 a month and only 5 blocks from the beach. Although the house was also in Ghost Town, the infamously druggie and dangerous section of Venice, I wasn't scared of street crime that much.

One night, Clair and Ennis had their first of many fights I witnessed that looked as if it was going to end up with Ennis punching Claire out. So I intervened, at which point Ennis told me he was going to get his gun [!] and gang [!!] and kill me [!!!!!]. I didn't move out immediately, because I didn't have the money to, and we kind of patched things up between us.

Well, that sort of opened the old floodgates and I got to know a darker and darker side of Ennis and Claire during the ensuing months that it took me to scrounge up enough funds to move out. Ennis was a bully and I was now one of his victims. This included him harassing me for rent before it was due, messing with my food and personal belongings, and telling me, "I can smell your fear." Ennis actually pissed in my orange juice… little did I know he was an aspiring mixologist. A man on the street does any of this to me and I open up restaurant kitchen-sized can whupass. But you can't react that way to people who can kill you in your sleep, or worse. I was really angry all the time.

I also didn't move out right away because Claire threw him out for a while, after he had destroyed her computer and put ink all over the clothing her closet… an inspiring fashion designer too, this Ennis was quite the Renaissance Man! I'm leaving a lot out, but I think you can tell what a classy guy Ennis was.

She confided in me, tearfully, "Ennis has never been anything but a bully his whole life, from day one." She seemed to know more about him than I did, most of it bad, but Claire was a very dumb and self-destructive evil cunt underneath her funny personality. She was more than happy to put people

68

in harms way of the boyfriend she knew was psychotic in order to pay her bills and get her mack on.

She took him back and Ennis resumed harassing me until I moved out with a very black cloud over my head. The next time I saw Ennis, we weren't gonna be roomies anymore, and he was going to meet A Whole New Patrick.

A few weeks after moving out, I saw Ennis and Claire on their bikes. They were at the beach where I played basketball and we had mutual friends. Ennis looked a little nervous. He was testing the waters of our new dynamic. I think he knew I wasn't going to let bygones be bygones. I should have just thrown him on his head and beat him until he was unconscious [or finally conscious] but instead I went up to him and whispered to him quietly:

"You need to get out of here or I am going to start beating the shit out of you. In fact, that goes for any place you see me for the rest of your life."

So Ennis began the charade that he played out at least a half-dozen times over the next three years. He got the fuck out of there and when he felt safe enough, he started hurling insults and threats at me. Seriously, it was like the guy was in first grade. Ennis wouldn't have lasted 10 minutes in Chicago. Some latter-day Leif Baio Twins would have filmed him being stomped by a 90s-era Erskine and have the video up on Youtube around the same time he was picking gravel out of his from an ass-whipping in the Scott back yard.

Any time I saw Ennis I gave him fair warning that he could either put an egg in his shoe and beat it, or win a thrilling trip for two to Fightey-Town. He always wisely chose option A.

I threw him out of a free concert at the Santa Monica pier, a drug store, Ralphs twice, and the same outdoor coffee shop three times. Seeing him just set me off. Ennis the bully was now Ennis the bitch, on

69

the run for talking his ass into a big problem that he couldn't solve with his usual dirtbag methods. And everyone knew it. Until my birthday, in January '07.

Boy, was I in good shape. Circuit weight training, basketball, volleyball, boxing, you name it. I was actually doing some personal training for friends as well. I was on my way to the beach to meet my client, riding my trusty bike, when I decided to stop for a taco at this place called Campos about a block from the sand. I entered and there was that dumb bitch Ennis and his trusty whore Claire. I guess Ennis was tired of running so he kind of got up and said something angrily as he walked toward me with fists all balled up. I cracked him. The perfect punch.

People don't go flying when they get punched, contrary to what you may have seen on Kung Fu Theater. Sometimes they buckle, sometimes they collapse, and sometimes they take a couple staggering steps, whatever.

Ennis went flying. It was the 600-foot home run ball that the batter never felt hit the bat. I literally didn't even feel the contact with him. It was like the wind went through him and his ass went flying until he skidded to a stop on his back.

Work done! I felt an immense sense of relief. Ennis was sort of the last grudge I was carrying around, so I felt like I could move on with my life as a peace-loving and productive citizen. I walked out onto the crowded street and was about to get on my bike when Ennis appears at the door of the taco Stand. He's about twenty feet from me and he's got a huge butcher knife in his hand. Same as the one featured in the movie, "Psycho."

He stops as he sees me turn toward him. Now, this is weird. This very dark part of me is actually glad that he's done this. Now I am going to kill him. I am going to take the knife from him and jam it up his ass. Literally. You hear that expression from time-

70

to-time, and I saw this as a golden opportunity to make it happen. From this day forth, Ennis could do his shit-talking, spliff-smoking skateboarding, threatening and lazing about attached to a colostomy bag.

There is a traffic cone nearby. I think about picking it up as a shield, but I am fairly and insanely confident that I can get the knife from him. I just have to get to his right wrist before he can jab me with it. Part of me is calculating that I am likely going to get cut badly on the forearm while doing this, but part of me is happy that he has now introduced the means to his own death into our duel.

I told you I am weird. But Ennis is a COMPLETE AND UTTER scumbag. I didn't even know to what extent he was abhorred until after all of this. SO MANY people came out with their Ennis stories. [A local bar owner said that Ennis had broken into his pub after hours and stolen guns from him and then threatened him after he was arrested for it. The police told me they arrested him constantly but had trouble making things stick and Ennis' **idiotic, asshole** mother always bailed him out and hired him an attorney.]

Ennis, the bitch-ass coward that he is and always will be, sees me advancing on him. Although he is armed with a deadly weapon, he runs back into the restaurant. I think, mistakenly, that he has no intention of using it, and that he has retreated to safety while awaiting my departure. He just had no intention of using it until I HAD MY BACK TURNED.

I gotta get out of here, I think. This has all the hallmarks of long and unpleasant questioning by the police, and I had just been sprung from jail for beating down that scumwad, Billy. I get on my bike and start pedaling away.

I hear Claire yell, "NOOO ENNIS," and this horrifying and astonishing heat fills the middle of my back in the shape of a long and flat triangle. I

71

know instantly that the butcher knife has gone through me, through me like a speared fish, like a Patrick-kabob. I feel an ocean of hot blood gushing inside me and I know that I am going to die very soon. That thought hits me like a black tidal wave of despair, and goes through every cell in my body, filling it with dread. And I gotta stop writing this.

FIGHTING TIP NUMBER NINE: Don't turn your back on a guy with a grudge, and a knife.

CHAPTER ELEVEN:
The Princess and the Pizza man.

"I have no trouble with my enemies. I can take care of my enemies in a fight. But my friends, my goddamned friends, they're the ones who keep me walking the floor at nights!" Warren G. Harding

During the years I lived in Laguna Beach, I was a total pussy. I was goaded into several fights that I backed down from and pretty much put the whole violence thing behind me. Probably because life was too effin' good. Which may give you [and me] some insight into the nature of violent people. I lived there after breaking up with my more-inland girlfriend, Sandy, in 1995. I was age 29 through 33, I never looked older than 25, and I always had a tan and sixpack abs. I was a good aspiring writer, a very good beach volleyballer, and pretty much always broke. But who cared?

I met this really cool girl from out of town named Julia on the Laguna Beach Boardwalk. She was 20 years old, very pretty and very funny. She had a great laugh, nice brown eyes, good legs and big cans. We went out, I took her back to my place and we had great sex.

At the time, I was working at this place with the unlikely name of Pizza Outlet, run by some very amusing guys from Jersey. I just remember Dutch, with his friendly attitude, can-do spirit, sweet black mullet and 25% stake in this fast food franchise with the dumbest name in the history of cuisine. Pizza Outlet?! Are you fucking kidding me?! Like they were a pie joint on the outskirts of town that sold all the badly-made pies, factory overruns and blemished pizzas the other franchises couldn't unload. Whatever. It paid my rent [barely] and fed me one giant pie per evening. Thank you, Dutch.

Anyway, the greatest thing about Julia was that she was so crazy about me she just wanted to ride along in the car with me when I delivered pizzas. Can you imagine that?

So one night she tells me that a guy I know from the beach has invited her to a party. A guy we all called "Fabio". Fabio's real name was Jeff and he sold pot at the beach and kept a lot of exotic animals at his house. He was also famous [or infamous] for owning this enormous exotic dog that once bit the shit out of his ex-girlfriend's face, tearing off her upper lip and requiring about 80 stitches. He was called Fabio because he had a good physique and long, bleached hair that had apparently never seen an ounce of conditioner. He was getting old and was usually found hitting unsuccessfully on younger women.

Jeff was something of a laughingstock. He was very chippy when it came to chicks. He had a boorish way of speaking about girls and *his game* was a little rusty, to say the least. He would get very petulant if he saw you talking to a girl that he saw first or had dibs on, or whatever. I was as worried about Julia falling for the likes of Fabio as I was about purchasing a comprehensive insurance policy for my barbecue grill.

Julia told me that Jeff had invited her to a party and wondered if I minded if she went with him. I didn't. I figured Fabio probably had shady motives but I was pretty secure. I mean this babe was doing pizza routes with me in my super-sweet 1981 Subaru mini wagon that I paid $300 for, in installments. Delivery routes for *Pizza Outlet,* no less.

I didn't really hang out with Jeff socially much if at all, but he seemed harmless.

Anyway, they go to this party, and this being an era when not *everyone* had a cell phone, I think I had to wait until the next day to get an update from Julia.

Old Fabio had NOT shown her a good time.

She tearfully told me that Jeff had gotten her in trouble with her dad by dumping her in the middle of nowhere and just throwing her backpack in the street after she had spurned his advances. Wow. There was more to it, but I had heard enough.

Boy, did I have to do a lot of psyching up to do what I did next. I hadn't fought anyone in maybe two years, and maybe four years before that, unless you count getting jumped. I knew that there was no question that I had to punch Jeff out. There was no debating it. But NONE of me really WANTED to. This would be a gruesome and dangerous chore to avenge the honor of sweet Julia. Jeff was no creampuff. I didn't think he was a fighter, but he clearly spent a lot of time at gym, even though much of it was likely blowing kisses in front of a mirror.

I really debated it all morning up until Jeff arrived at the beach around 1pm. I had to do it. He had disrespected a great girl and made a mockery out of me in the process.

He was eating his lunch, sitting on the boardwalk that is about two or three feet above the sand. It was a hot and sunny day with lots and lots of people around. I gathered up all my courage, I walked up behind him and said, "Jeff, we have to talk." Jeff said:

"Yeah, well go ahead and talk."

"You are going to want to stand up for what I am about to say..."

He reluctantly got up and turned to face me and I said,

"You got this coming."

I swung and kinda missed or he blocked it. Now, I hadn't trained or hit anything so much as a bag for years, so that likely had something to do with my accuracy problem. Well, that didn't go as planned.

So we struggled for a second and some part of me remembered a long-ago wrestling maneuver called the double-leg takedown. You just drop down and shoot in, grab you opponent behind the knees, pick him up and slam him to the mat.

But behind Jeff there was no mat. There was that three-foot drop-off and we both go flying down. I made sure I landed with all my body weight [maybe 185 at that time] square on top of him. He kind of got me in headlock from the ground, and I told him if he let me go that I would let him up without punching him. Jeff had big biceps, and was holding on with all he had. I was shocked that he was still fighting after the fall. We were separated and I left the beach.

The locals were kind of horrified that I had done this. It wasn't the vibe people down there dug at all. Jeff was quite a little politician, but everyone also was aware that he was a creep, so they probably knew that he was lying about his version of the events that provoked me: Jeff said it was all a "big misunderstanding", the type you might see on the show, "Three's Company". Oops, there goes Jack Tripper tossing some chick out of his car in the middle of the night, what are the Ropers going to think about that!?

Julia and I parted ways the next day, promising to stay in touch... we didn't.

I saw Jeff in a parking lot later that month at a local grocery store. He postured with some aggressive talk and I said:

"You want round two? I am happy to oblige you." I wasn't really happy to, but it seemed to be the right thing to say.

He made placating gestures and switched his tactic. He said he couldn't believe that I would

believe some chick I just met over him, and this
'bros before hos' nonsense, and then he described how
I had severely exacerbated an existing back problem
he had [good!], and had damaged a bulging disc or
whatever. I didn't really feel that sorry for him or
completely buy his story, but I was happy to have
peace at the beach again. It was never really brought
up again. I moved out of Laguna in 1999.

AFTERWARD
Sometime in 2006, I went to my favorite bar, The
Brig [obviously before I was 86'd for life for
breaking Cappy's face]*.

I was kind of hitting on this girl when we both
realized that we looked familiar. I think it dawned
on me first... it was Julia. We had a lot of laughs
and reminisced about the good times. She admitted to
me that she was 18 at the time and had lied about her
age. She had just recently moved from New Jersey to
LA and was editing film and really happy and
successful [at least one of us was]. Then I brought
up Jeff, and was getting ready to laugh about
breaking his bad back when her mood suddenly
darkened.

She then proceeded to tell me some revealing ugly
details about that night with Jeff. Had I known this
at the time, I would have been intent on killing him
rather than merely punching him out. Use your
imagination.

Uh-oh, Chrissy and Janet are going to be pissed!
Gee Fabio, you better hope that these little tidbits
don't circulate around The Regal Beagle!

CHAPTER TWELVE:
WHY WE FIGHT
[The Circle Bar Fight]

"Don't hit at all if it is honorably possible to avoid it, but never hit soft."
-Teddy Roosevelt

"Why We Fight," by the way, is the name of one of the episodes of the super-stellar mini-series, "Band of Brothers". That episode was about the allied troops discovering the first Nazi death camp and how that made fighting Hitler worth all the bloodshed. The complete and utter irony of naming this chapter the same thing about an insanely stupid fistfight is intentional.

I get harassed more than others do at bars. Ask anyone who knows me. Even my most exasperated friends, who have believed I am at least partially at fault for all my fights, usually have their disbelief and skepticism suspended after going out with me once or twice. I am simply a hater magnet.

I also spend an inordinate amount of time in bars. At least half the time, I go by myself. That's two ways being in harms way. AND, I also am almost always found talking to a girl. I am maybe even *overly* friendly and sociable even when I am not trolling. I look like a sheltered white guy. Maybe I have the kind of face that people want to punch. Another person had an insight as well, he thought: Maybe you look like a guy who WILL fight, and some of these people are insane or masochistic and they are just looking for a co-dependent, I don't know, violent dumbass.

Whatever the reason, I can't stand it. AND I am absolutely PSYCHIC when it comes to avoiding trouble. I can spot an obnoxious overbearing A-hole in a crowded bar from MILES away [special thanks the brand Ed Hardy for making this process immensely easier]. I usually get to know the security staff at any bar I frequent. When I spot a troublemaker, I'll go over and alert the bouncers. I did that just last night. Because even if he is currently badgering someone else, I know this asshole will get around *to bothering me* eventually.

Knowing this, I have developed a series of "deflector shields", or tactics I use to channel aggressive energy away from me like a ninja. At least twenty times a year, a guy will come up to me and say something completely idiotic, such as:

[Mocking tone] "Hey guyssss, ITS TROY AIKMAN, HEY ITS TROY AIKMAN!"

[To girl I am talking with, interrupting our conversation] "You shouldn't be talking to this guy, he's too good-looking for you, he's just going to use you."

"Dude, you look a little old to be in this club, how old are you?"

"Hey, what's up, Hasselhoff."

"Hey, dude, no way are you talking to these chicks, its not going to happen." [The girls don't know this person]

In the words of our awesome president Barack Obama; "ENOUGH!"

One of my all-purpose lines for the guy who asks me how old I am or has a smart-ass comment about my clothing or whatever is:

"Sorry, I'm here to meet girls, there are several gay clubs in the area, though."

This has a HILARIOUS effect, always. They start sputtering about how they are not gay and I ask them then why are they talking to me in a bar packed with women. ["Real", or out-of-the-closet gays are the only polite subgroup I can think of, possibly besides non-incarcerated Mexicans, in Los Angeles.]

In the 'Hasselhoff' commentary, I would just pretend to get on my cell phone and say, "Yeah, I gotta go, this bar is filled with assholes."

ASIDE: I was in Home Depot one afternoon and I went up to a guy who was standing near the paint counter, practically behind it, he looked a bit like a meth head. I politely asked him where the WD-40 was and he became apoplectic with anger: "I don't work here, I don't work at fuckin Home Depot… STUPID!" The "stupid" really tore it. I couldn't figure out what to do so I sidle up next to him and his girlfriend as they are checking out and I say the following into my phone [to nobody]: **"NO, I DIDN'T GET MAD, I SHOULD HAVE REALIZED THE GUY LOOKED TOO STUPID TO HAVE A JOB."** I looked at him pointedly. He wilted. As I walked out I saw him trying to explain what had just happened to his girl.

I could go on and on. As any girl in LA will tell you, the town is packed with very aggressive, annoying, sexually frustrated guys with chips the size of cement blocks on their shoulders.

Well, whatever. I **am** patient, but sometimes I lose it.

I don't have any idea if I am still a community hazard because I haven't fought anyone for almost two years, but there have been times in my life where I was an out-and-out **dangerous** person to pick a fight with - for some people anyway. Big deal, right? Well, it IS kind of a big deal when some overconfident frat boy is humiliating you, challenging you, punking you out, and you know that HE KNOWS it isn't worth your time or effort to get physical. BUT IT KILLS YOU when you know how stupid it is that some guy is pushing a thousand dollars worth of Health Insurance chips [yours and his] to earn ten cents worth of swelling in his balls, just because nobody has ever busted his bubble yet. But it doesn't mean that nobody ever will. I have taken a completely nonsensical, self-destructive and Pyrrhic sense of pride in sometimes being That Guy. The Ace of Spades in the pack of Old Maid cards.

Which leads up to Chapter 6's Why We fight Tale. Another pointless tale of Horrifying Injury to a an annoying schmuck who provoked the wrong guy.

Circle Bar Fight

The Circle bar is a chill bar in Santa Monica. It's called the Circle Bar because the bar is in the middle and you kind of mill around in a circle eyeballing the objects of your affections. The bar is usually well represented by drunk females in an amorous mood. Good times. But it also tends to get very crowded and it's tough to navigate around that loop, so sometimes tempers run short. They have an outstanding security staff to handle these matters.

It, like the Brig, went through a makeover when Venice Beach's transformation from Druggy Beachside Hellhole to Hipster Heaven evolved from 1960 to the present. The Circle Bar, hilariously, never completely got rid of the barf smell that haunted the place like a stinky poltergeist despite its upscale makeover.

So I'm walking through the bar and I get this really hard two-hand shove in the small of my back. I turn to try to figure out what happened and I see this medium-sized guy shoving the hell out of me. I just said something placating like, "hey slow down, relax, man."

"OOOOOOOH, are you some kind of tough guy!??? **You** relax, buddy… just keep walking if you know what's good for you." He shoved me **again.**

JE-SUS CHRIST! I'm not even looking at this guy and he has shoved and threatened me in less than five seconds. GODDAMMIT, that shows how fast a-holes roll up on you in LA, I mean, this NEVER happened to me in Chicago and it's probably happened at least twenty times a year in LA. [Admittedly, this is on the high side because I spend all my time, money, youth, etc. at pubs.]

I try to be a patient man, but you know, this guy was obviously going around the bar looking for trouble, and you know what, he found some. I don't think I made any preamble. OK, maybe I am not that patient of a man every single time.

"Perhaps you would like to step outside?"

Well, he did. But a curious thing happened when Mr. Bully McIdiot got outside… and this has happens often. Some very primitive part of his puny brain has sounded a warning bell. We step outside and he says:

"Hey, bro, I don't even remember what we were fighting about." Oh, here we go. Gee, it was all so long ago, like forty-five seconds. A faded Polaroid gathering dust in a long-forgotten dresser drawer.

I have heard this SO MANY TIMES. But I am not taking the dangerous step of walking outside to kinda "see where this goes." But guys try to back out after going "all in" all the time.

It may have something to do with my appearance. If you don't look at me very carefully, you probably see spoiled white boy, surfer, whatever. In the uncomfortable moments before a fight, there can be a less careless assessment going on. I'm good-sized, not ripped but strong-looking… maybe like a 1950s-era movie Tarzan, and I have had a few people tell me that I look a little crazy. I also, whenever possible, do almost no talking before a fight, because I am assessing my opponent's weak points like he is a Bad Robot that I am going to have to de-activate. Anyway, a guy wants out? I usually just breathe a sigh of relief and go back to whatever it was that I was doing.

But *this time* I just said what was on my mind.

"Oh, I remember, you want a re-cap? You shoved me real hard, when *I politely* pointed it out, you called me a tough guy, so I asked you to back it up and now we are out here and you are acting like a pussy. *Because you are a pussy.* You go around picking fights with people and then you are such a fucking punk you can't even back your own mouth, bitch. Now you know, so suck on that." Or some pleasantries to that effect. At least I felt better as I turned on my heel smartly and strolled back into the bar. I wish I had done the Willy Wonka line, which I remembered to do at some later confrontation: "I bid you GOOD DAY, SIR!!!"

You have to understand, when you are trolling for babes and having beers with friends, you are pretty far from a violent headspace. I had left the house starring in my own romantic comedy and now I was being forced into the leading role of a dangerous and pointless documentary.

I had to calm down and try to reboot my evening again, which isn't that easy, but I was starting to manage a positive buzz after about ten minutes of deep breathing and a couple brewskis. I was with my very funny friend Yoji. I didn't even tell him what happened, as it didn't even dignify repeating.

BUT DICKHEAD'S LITTLE PEABRAIN STARTED CHEWING ON THE WORDS I had said, and he apparently found them hard to digest. I kept an eye on him; he was on the other side of the bar, ruminating and stewing, about to make an incredibly bad decision. He walked back up to me with a friend in tow and said, "You know what, I think I'd like to have that fight with you now."

FUUUUUUUUUUUUUUUUUUCKSTICKS!!!!

Man, was I PISSED. OFF. Dark and black anger was welling around. COME TO THE DARRK SI-IDE LUKE. Now I have to fight, put myself at physical risk, oooh because this guy liked to start fights in bars for

84

[fun?] RRRRRRRRRRRR. Well, he shoulda listened to his Smart Side, that's for sure. He just took the batteries out of his smoke alarm right before his house caught fire. I'm broiling-mad now.

Despite the lighthearted tone of these essays, I don't really take fighting lightly. It's serious business. I would say in at least half of my last ten fights, someone required medical attention or hospitalization. It's not like getting a bloody lip over a fight at the drinking fountain and getting grounded from the jungle gym for a month. Adult fights can get hairy as hell. Some people said it was only a matter of time before I killed someone. I was never worried about that, for troublemakers have surprisingly thick skulls. They have to. I don't have a lot of extra money, so I don't even like getting my clothes ripped up. And even when you win, you often hurt your back or sprain your wrist.

Anyway, his asshole buddy is with him now, his Bundini Brown. "Oh dude, he is going to kill you, bro this is going to be sooo funny, you are making the biggest mistake of your life," etc. etc.

It was a little unnerving because obviously my opponent had some experience and I was also worried about this other joker jumping in. I may also be too drunk to fight at full speed. No backing out now.

I told my friend Yoji, who is a really strong guy but not a fighter, to make sure nobody jumped in, especially his little cheerleader. The bouncers just tell us not to do it in front of the bar and a little crowd has gathered by now. He does something that worries me a little: He drops into a fighting stance.

Most guys don't. They just stand there yelling at you with little targets painted all over them. So he knows how to fight. Which probably made what happened next worse for him, because that stance got my attention.

WE circle each other for what seemed to be a pretty long time and he finally throws a couple punches. As he comes forward I grabbed his left arm in what is known in wrestling as an arm drag. You basically use the person's momentum to drag them past you and then you are behind them where you can lock your hands around their waist and throw them to the mat. But there was no mat out there. There never is, by the way, for all of you that think your Fighting Aerobics classes have taught you how to defend yourselves outside a bar.

There was, however, a brick wall that I dragged him by the arm into. I then grabbed his head and slammed it into the wall a couple times. It's never like one of those silly Jackie Chan movies where dudes just go flying and you hit them with garbage can lids [Jackie Chan is a very funny and acrobatic dude, but if you think for a second any of that bullshit would fly in a real fight then you are trippin']. He resisted my slamming his head into the wall, but his head definitely got knocked a few times. It hit him hard enough to jar his equilibrium so I could spin him back the other way and slam him on his back, making sure, GENTLE READER, that his head hit the curb. He was still struggling! I was **amazed** that he was still conscious [Remember what I said about fight-picker-guys' hard heads, sheesh.] So I then dialed up two nasty rights into his face. Those bounced his head off the curb and he screamed for help as he went limp.

Damn. It was a little much, but I have to bring the old hossenfeffer until they don't fight back. No reason for me to get hurt or get my church slacks torn up. It wasn't <u>my idea in the first place</u> to start trouble, you know? I got up and so, miraculously did he, to **amazingly talk more shit** [they are a different breed I tells ya]. I think he was letting the assembled onlookers know that he wasn't hurt and that I hit like a girl or something.

Then all of a sudden he collapsed into a heap in the middle of his speech, which drastically undermined its intended impact. He mumbled a couple things up from the sidewalk like a broken doll that still has that string you can pull to make it talk.

He was like that knight in "Monty Python's Holy Grail" who is still talking trash with his arms and legs cut off. [I remember a fight at the Venice hoops courts where a guy got knocked out for talking shit and they carried him to the bleachers. He woke up a few minutes later and resumed his tirade, and then the *same guy* had to knock him out **again.**]

His friend helped him up and dragged him away like a guy helping an injured player off a football field. I forgot to ask him if this was how his friend kicked ass. He probably told the asshole that I suckered him with a lucky punch and they could be back out bothering people just as soon as his CAT scan came back negative.

I'm guessing he sustained a concussion at least. I'm sure he woke up with noisy fluid draining in his sinus cavity for at least a few days. Making that scary ticking noise that fighters know. Maybe not. No brain, no headache.

I wondered for a while after that fight if the guy had permanent damage or something. It was a very savage beat down. I wasn't THAT worried. I mean, the guy had chosen a very risky and stupid hobby. Do you really feel sorry for the for the guy who guy who handles rattlesnakes and then gets bitten to death? That's some Darwinism going on there, you know?

The other thing was, after the fight, it took me like an hour to catch my breath.

I made a mental note to work on the old cardio.

CHAPTER THIRTEEN:
THROUGH THE LOOKING GLASS WEIRD

GETTING JUMPED, PART ONE

I got jumped for the first time in the summer of 1987, visiting my friend who attending Michigan State. The jumping part was weird, but what happened during it even weirder.

It was a warm summer night and I was out by myself on the porch of his rented student shack located in the student ghetto when I hear a woman's cry for help. I go out to the street and the girl is just sitting in the driver's side of a beat-up car and three dudes get out. One circles behind me while the other two stand in front. One of the guys is short, practically a midget. Angry midget. I instantly realized that I was the victim of some skeevy little set-up. The girl wails, the unwitting Good Samaritan runs out and the three guys beat him up and rob him or whatever. Shits and giggles. Uh oh.

The guy is now behind me and the little guy just charges me as fast as he can and tackles me at the waist. I get a grip on his hair and use him as a shield to jam the other two. I spin away and run up the stairs, they are in hot pursuit.

There is a full-sized axe on the front porch.

I pick it up and turn. Swear to God, the weirdest thing happened. I become another person.

It was like when I reached for the axe I was a scared-to-death child and when I picked it up I was a rather jolly 45-year-old with a very avuncular attitude towards killing. This new persona was about as worried about the current situation as you might be getting ready to eat the cookies grandma was getting out of the oven. He [I] turned to face the midget with a half-smile on my face. He pretended to

89

go for a gun in his jacket. I knew he didn't have it. I walked toward him.

I planned to chop him through his collarbone, hitting him with only about an inch of the axe head, just the tip, as the ladies say. That way he would be out of commission and I would still have the axe to use. If I was to fully chop into him like a tree, it was a good chance the axe would get stuck and I wouldn't have it for the other two. Axe-murdering 101, but how the hell would I know something like that?

They ran away, but left me with a very weird memory.

"If you let a bully come in your front yard, he'll be on your porch the next day and the day after that he'll rape your wife in your own bed."
-Lyndon B. Johnson

"I had my bully, and it was excruciating. Not only the bully, but the intimidation I felt."
- Robert Cormier

Lisa: [about Bobby] He treats everyone like shit. He's always mean. He's always cruel. He beats you up.

Lisa: [laughs] He's even too weird for Ali and she's into everything!   He's the source of everybody's troubles, Marty.   And even still, he's going to finish high school and go to college and probably get rich.

Marty: Yeah, and I'm going to be delivering pizzas to him in Weston. How would we get a gun?
- Dialog from the [excellent] film "Bullies"

MAN, DO I KNOW a lot about bullies. Schoolyard bullies, financial bullies, family bullies, office bullies, whatever. Why me, you ask. It's because I have been pretty much broke for twenty years. Like those poor farmers Clint Eastwood saves in westerns can tell you, bullies fuck with the poor. However, unlike those sharecroppers, my poverty had a lot to do with the fact that I spent my rent money on booze and good times. *"Hey stranger, thanks for shooting that crooked land baron, would you mind clearing out for a couple hours, I got chicks coming over to the cabin, no they are both for me and they are bringing E so can I borrow two bits and your Palomino to pick them up?"*

Basically, a bully likes to do things outside the rules because they get what they want without having to wait or pay. They live in the Bully Express lane.

Some bullies do very well financially. They live in a world few of us understand. My bastardized existence has put me in the path of a lot of them.

Some societies are much more accepting of the bully mentality… many Middle Eastern countries go by the Might Is Right way of doing things, and you can see the peace and joy that has brought them. We Americans pride ourselves on fairness, and fairness is kryptonite to a bully. Jerome Bettis, the great Pittsburgh Steeler running back, said he came home from being bullied one day at school and his mama told him the only way to deal with a bully: punch him in the mouth. He did, and it worked! I think we, as a people, make the mistake of trying to reason with bullies like Dick Cheney, for instance.

Bullies know the TERRAIN of danger and physical and or emotional violence, because that's where they live. Normal people don't understand that. "Why did he hit you? You MUST have done something to antagonize him." Maybe not. The bully just thought he could get away with it.

Let me give you a very typical bullying situation: I am drinking by myself at the Brig and I meet a very cute girl. Two ass-biters tell me to stop talking to her. I ask the girl if she knows these guys and she says she does not. I tell them to fuck off. They tell me they are going to beat me up. "The two of you?" They both nod like a couple smartasses. They are medium-sized, not easy pickins like the two little Chicanes in jail.

Two guys step up behind me. They have heard the whole conversation.

"We got your back."

Wow, I can't believe two guys in LA are doing this for me. Turns out they are from out of town [Minnesota], of course. So I say:

"You heard him, so which one of you two pussies is going to get it first?"

They immediately start running around and crying like little girls, they go and get the bouncer and tell him the mean and scary Patrick is after them. I mean they just changed gears so fast, without any thought. IT'S BECAUSE BULLIES DO THIS SHIT ALL THE TIME. They are well-acquainted with the terrain. Bully, presto chango, victim.

I'll tell you, there are few things more satisfying than the look on a bully's face when they realize they are in way over their head. Bullies make up a small percentage of the population but they leave a huge footprint. More than once, I have left a bully in a state of disarray outside a club and people come up and say, "Hey, thanks for doing that, the guy was bothering us all night." You and everyone else he meets.

A PERFECT example of a local bully gone wild was this jerkoff that I worked for. Chip and I got the job installing cabinets for this kind of beefy guy with red hair and a walrus mustache named Reed. Reed gave us a set of plans and we began to hang the cabinets in a kitchen somewhere near Long Beach. About two hours in, Reed unleashes this weird and abusive tirade at one of his employees:

"WHAT THE FUCK, ARE YOU ON CRACK? YOU ARE LIKE A FUCKIN THIRD-GRADER. CAN'T YOU GET ANY OF THIS SHIT RIGHT, YOU STUPID MOTHERFUCKER."

His employee did the appropriate shaking and quaking that prolly gave old Reed a "good-sized wood."

Now Reed wasn't talking to Chip and me; he was going off on a member of his own crew. But I was pretty sure he would get around to us. We needed the money, but I would smoke Reed like a candy cigarette if he said any of that shit to me, and I didn't need any more drama in my life.

His dumbass plans were wrong so we were going to have to redo the cabinets. But we told Reed we'd rather just get paid for the day and leave it at that. He thought about it, his little bully brain working, and told us that he would come back with cash in "two shakes." I asked him how long it was going to take and he said, "as long as it takes to get to Wells Fargo and back."

Reed never returned with our money. Fuck. We kept asking his crew where the fuck he went because he wouldn't answer his cell phone. We got burnt.

Chip came up with the bright idea to pretend to leave for a half hour or so and then come back. He was obviously getting reports from his crew that we were still there.

We split for a little bit and then came back. There was old Reed, working in the back yard with his crew of four or five guys. As I walked up, he was scraping the paint off a door jamb.

"Hey, Reed, where's our money?"

"Well, I gotta talk to you about that-"

"There's no talking Reed, you said you went to get our money, dodged our calls and now you are back. Where is it?"

Reed puffed up his porky barrel ass to its full 5'11" and said, "You better calm down, or that mouth of yours is going to get you in trouble."

See this is where the college-looking guy starts sputtering and apologizing and not wanting to get his ass kicked by an OG like Reed. Reed took a threatening step toward me just for effect. Oh gosh.

Again, I had done some rapid calculations. Reed was big, but not that big. He maybe had me by ten or fifteen pounds, all of that lard. There was no way he was stronger than me, and no way he was faster either. I also had height, experience and range on him. Old Reed had gone through too many hot dogs, Hot Pockets and nights watching Girls Gone Wild tapes while I was working out and hitting the wrestling mat that I had nailed to the tree outside my apartment.

"Dude, if you walk up on me I am going to choke you out right here in front of your boys." I said this with a pleasant smile.

It was pretty funny because his footstep stopped in the air like we were playing Freeze Tag.

"Get your fuckin wallet out and give us our money."

"Well, you ah, don't know who you're ah."

"What Reed? You are a fucking bitchass bully. We heard the way you talked to your crew earlier. **God** put me here to kick your ass in front of your crew, you see how they aren't doing anything? Its cuz they want it to happen. Do something, bitch." I knew I wasn't going to get paid, so I was determined to take my 200 bones out of his Jimmy Dean's pork sausage ass. I couldn't think of anything to egg him on. Then a weird thought hit me. Reed was undoubtedly a racist, sooo:

"You know what you are Reed? You are acting like a chickenshit nigger."

Gentle Reader, you are now putting down the book, ashamed to be reading the words of some Klan representative. OK, what I said is **never right**, but I wanted Reed to fight me SO BADLY. I knew he was one of those redneck contractors, and I also knew calling him a nigger in front of his boys would sting for a hundred years. Forgive me ghost of MLK, my heart was in the right place. It was wrong.

95

You should have heard his boys suck all the air out of the backyard when I laid that little H-bomb on him. I thought for sure that if anything would make him "feel froggy and jump," that would be it.

Reed was too smart for that. The old catfish looked at the lure and went straight to the bottom. Bullies are VERY cagey. He knew if he actually stepped up, he was going to end up a bloody mess. He took his fat ass and walrus stash into the house, locked the door and said he was calling the cops. WHAT A PUNK!!!!

Oh well, we left without our money. But I sent Chip in to be the good cop to my bad cop [sorry, you don't know Pat, he's plum crazy, he'll come and kill you, I'm sorry] and he collected maybe half our money. Chip was all excited. He claimed what had happened looked like a deleted scene from "Tombstone."

I have collected money from abusive and bullying landlords and bosses for people. Just for the fun of it. I love watching a bully squirm.

I worked for this other bully named Bill when I lived on the docks in Marina Del Rey. Bill had this amazing yacht that was from 1920 and was like 80 feet long and he needed portions of it painted for a video shoot. I had already heard about Bill's rather famous bullying. He threw this cool guy Axel into the water and had done some other creepy stuff. I needed the dough. He had brown hair, he was about forty-five and had a push broom moustache. I found out later he owed money to everyone in the world, had been thrown out of the yacht club for picking fights, and had tortured his ex-wife by tying her to a bed and pouring ice water on her. This chhaaaaraarming man!!

Bill was a big sonofabitch at 6'3" and a very beefy 240. He had hired me for $12.50 an hour. This was the work I was doing at age 38 as a failed [temporarily] writer. Stay in school kids.

Bill seemed pretty cool at first, always making jokes, but kind of bagging on us to work faster. But I'm a pretty fast worker anyway. He also hired some day laborers and spoke pretty decent Spanish with them. His diet was funny; he would just cook this humongous steak on his barbecue grill and eat it with chili. That's all he ever ate. The Anger Diet Plan.

So after working for him one day, the day laborer asks where is his money and Bill tells him he's going to drop it off for him TOMORROW at Home Depot. Who does that? You shouldn't need a signed contract as a day laborer [I have been one, stay in school kids]. Everyone knows you pay the day laborer AT THE END OF THE COCKADOODY DAY!

So I say, "Yo Bill, when is payday around here anyway?"

"It's when I say it is, get back to work!"

Silence. AARE YOUUUU KIDDING MEE?

"Bill, I know you are joking."

We get into this long argument and I know he's over a barrel with the deadline so I tell him that I will only continue to work for him if he pays me up to date. He agrees, telling me that my reputation has been severely damaged forever. Sure, dude.

He returns in a snit with the cash and I consider slinking off but I don't. I pocket the money and I look him in the eye and say:

"I don't care how much you paid me, I'd never work another minute for an asshole like you." I assume I'm going to get him to swing on me, and I'm ready. Although I am standing casually, I have my weight loaded up on my back foot ready to knock him silly with a huge right.

But being a BULLY, he knows how to only take the easy fights and since I don't have 'Easy Fight'

97

written all over me, he throws a few insults my way about being dishonorable while backing away carefully like a raccoon retreating from your trash can.

For months after that, I used to get drunk and go down to his boat, call him a bitch and call him out. Once he even had a date over and I told her about how he beat women. I was a major thorn in his side for a while until I bored with tormenting the big bully.

Sorry there were no actual fights there, folks, I tried, but bullies are cagey as hell. Maybe now I'll tell you about the second beatdown I laid on that scumbag Billy. A bully I did get my hands on!

FIGHTING TIP NUMBER EIGHT: TAKE ADVANTAGE OF THE FIRST CHANCE YOU GET TO UNLOAD ON A BULLY. IT WILL PROBABLY BE YOUR ONLY CHANCE.

CHAPTER FIFTEEN:
BILLY, WARRIOR PRINCESS, PART DOS

"Cowards are cruel, but the brave have mercy and delight to save."
-John Gay

"And the King shall answer and say unto them, Verily I say unto you, Inasmuch as ye have done [it] unto one of the least of these my brethren, ye have done [it] unto me."
-The Bible

WELL, IF you were worried that I did any permanent damage to BILLY, WARRIOR PRINCESS by grabbing him by his ponytail and slamming his caveman head on the ground, you can relax. He was back on his feet and acting stupid within no time. I heard from other sources that after I slammed his misshapen Cro-Magnon cranium on the ground, he staggered in and *ordered coffee,* just to prove he wasn't shattered by the savage beating! Guy should be in Ripley's Believe it Or Not. I told you about the thick skulls of villains already. A normal guy, like a schoolteacher or web page designer, you slam his skull on the sidewalk like that, he's going to be in bed with an ice bag on it for a week. Not old Billy, Warrior Princess. He takes a lickin and keeps on tickin! You know, like that cockroach you have to step on four times and spray with Raid and it still scampers under the baseboards where it probably talks shit at you that you can't hear ["You stomp like my girlfriend!"].

Billy was very angry and veklempt about what had happened so he did some really stupid things to try to unnerve me. He used to park his truck outside my house just to show me he was around and not afraid of me. Then he and his brother chased me around for a while in his truck while I was on my bike.

99

Funny, a few days later I run into his runty brother *without* Billy at a pizza place and I asked him to step outside and boy, you never saw such a 180 in all your life... I didn't *understand*, Billy was at church the day the homeless guy got beat down and they were just trying to flag me down to try to tell me that. They were just trying to EXPLAIN that to me. Don't you see? I let him know that I didn't believe him and that he had just narrowly escaped a world-class stomping, and I split.

It was a bad decision on my part not to slam *his* head onto the sidewalk a few times as well. I should have offered him the family plan: Unlimited weekday head slams for a small monthly fee, evening and weekend beatdowns were, of course free... not including any unused rollover punchouts.

I was really exhausted by all of this. You would think a grown man would have better things to do with his time, but I kind of felt that The Lord kept putting this guy in front of me.

Later that month, on Abbot Kinney Boulevard, I actually had a fight with Billy, his dirtbag girlfriend, and his brother. The girl came up and grabbed my bike and the brother had something to say, too. They were going to call the cops and hold me accountable for the original coffee shop incident. Billy got old Peppercalibur out and this time got some on my neck. The guy got his trusty canister out faster than Wild Bill Hickock. He probably had been practicing his quick draw in the mirror.

Even though they outnumbered me three-to-one, the guys kept their distance and let the chick do the heavy lifting by wrestling me for my bike. This was turning into a no-net, highwire white trash circus mishap that results in fatality. I never wanted have such a close relationship with these three lowlife drug addict pieces of shit. What the hell were they living in Venice for anyway? Wasn't there a desert town with crystal meth labs everywhere with their names on it? I couldn't picture them splashing

100

around in the surf in their biker boots, dirty jeans and black concert t-shirts.

It was funny, after this incident, a guy told me that outside the original beatdown coffee shop location, he saw Billy, Warrior Princess threaten to take a swing at his chick, who was often seen sporting a black eye. This guy was truly a cultured aristocrat!

It all came to a close at Ralphs market on Lincoln. Billy walked in without the protection of his runty brother, beat-up cunt girlfriend or his fabled mist of mace-y mayhem, Peppercalibur. I was walking past the check stands at the front of the store when Billy walked in. I advanced toward him wordlessly, like The Terminator.

He said, "Hey man, we ain't doin this now." *Aren't* doing this now, Billy, it's "aren't."

I didn't say anything. I just walked up and grabbed him and started swinging him around.

I don't think I did much physical damage to the creep, but damn, it was fun. Like something you would see in the movies. Tossed him through like a wine display endcap and then something else. CRASH! All these bottles are flying everywhere. I think I dumped him over that place where they sell you flowers and balloons and wrecked that. Come to think of it, it WAS like the scene in "The Terminator" where Arnie throws that dude around the apartment.

Although I loves me my Ralphs, it was delightful to use Billy's head to bust up their store. I ended the fight by throwing him on the ground and punching him in his face. Ah, seems like old times. If he had used his Ralph's card for this ass kicking, he could have saved money on his next one.

I split, ironically telling Billy, "Peace out."

NOT DISPLAYING THE INTELLIGENCE of a 5-time Jeopardy! Champ, I returned to the store a few

101

minutes later to retrieve the cell phone I dropped in the melee, only to be arrested and put in L.A. County Jail for stalking, on $150,000 bail. That little bitch had reported all of our fights, even though he had started them all. And Gentle Reader, L.A. County Jail makes Orange County Jail seem like a Pleasant Hawaiian vacation.

AFTERWARD:

The day Billy and his old lady showed up in court to get his restraining order, Billy wore like the dirtiest t-shirt you ever saw. I started humming, "Every girl crazy bout a sharp-dressed man." The judge gave him his restraining order. Oh well. I was getting tired of beating his skull, which was four inches thick. In the long run, it didn't do either one of us any good. But at least the cops said nice things about me after I almost croaked.

CHAPTER SIXTEEN:
HOOP COURT FIGHT

A COUPLE funny things about this fight: One thing is that it seems like an out and out miracle that I only had one fight at the full-court hoops section of the Venice Beach Recreation Center, AKA Muscle Beach; and the other is that it's not fitting that I would devote a chunk of this book to write about a negative incident at a location that provided me with virtually unlimited entertainment, laughter, camaraderie, lifelong friendships and flat-out incredible basketball games with some of the greatest street ballers ever!

You may have seen OUR COURT immortalized in the opening scenes of the very funny "White Men Can't Jump" where dueling midgets Wesley Snipes and Woody Harrelson dunked on a seven-foot hoop. Ah, the magic of Hollywood. You may have also seen the courts depicted in an insufferable scene in "American History X," where a racist and muscle-bound, five-foot-eight Ed Norton dunks off a slightly off-screen ladder, cherry picker or trampoline. He then tells "the niggers that they can't play there anymore. SHEEEEEEEEEEEEYAAAAAA, RIGHT!!!

For the record, I am an Ed Norton fan, but even his considerable acting skills couldn't sell this lazily-researched and reality-free scenario. Maybe you could tell all the niggers in Venice, ITALY, to get off their own basketball court, providing they didn't understand a single word of English. I will venture to guess in the history of outdoor pick-up game hoops, no group of white supremacists has ever gone to a predominately black court and said "boo," much less telling all the "niggers to go home."

Your Gentle Author, with fighting skills detailed ad nauseum for your reading pleasure, about whom this hilarious black guy JT once pronounced humorously, "Pat been accepted by the black community," never even came close to using the n-word, even though it constituted a good 10% of the vernacular there. [Nigga, you must trippin, nigga, that ain't a foul, check BALL, nigga! [The preceding could even be addressed to ME]]

That court was not for the weak or faint of heart. Some Saturdays, it looked like a basketball game with 9 guys from the Grambling football team and one lifeguard, if I was playing. It was an incredibly fast and athletic run, with antelope-like fast breaks, soaring dunks, nasty collisions and arguments that sometimes lasted an hour and a half. We all were performers who LOVED the fact that big crowds would watch us play. In a weird way, the court was a perfect fit for me. I was a baller of medium skills that could pass, dribble, and shoot an occasional three, but I had a bachelor's degree in defense, rebounding and chasing down loose balls, with a PhD in heckling the games I wasn't playing in. One guy named G said I played basketball as if it was rugby and added, "You don't see a bunch a black people goin' down to YOUR neighborhood and fuckin' up a hockey game, Pat."

I liked the fact that it was a rougher game. I was comfortable with the threat of violence that sometimes hung in the air. And, as you might have guessed, I could talk some trash, too. I don't remember saying it, but Chip told me that one big black guy had a problem with my physical play and threatened me. I reportedly told him, "If you don't want anyone playing defense on you, you can come back out and play by yourself after sundown." I had the privilege of being threatened by some of the most feared dudes in LA. Maybe it distracted me from the fact that the rest of my life was such a bloody car wreck that was going nowhere.

I think part of me wanted that eventual fight. I got threatened, cheated and punked out of my game so many times as a [sob] minority, that I was getting an itchy trigger finger. I realized that most of the guys were better basketball players than me, had grown up in rougher areas and had the backing of their boys, but I kind of felt if the shit went down, I could surprise somebody with a different athletic skill set: My squabbling skilz.

I probably became overconfident and squared up on some dudes that might have really punched my ticket. I think some of the guys were a little more leery of fighting me because I was such an unknown quantity.

I certainly didn't start any trouble, but when threatened physically, I adopted a standard approach. I would just say calmly, "Don't threaten me" or "Check ball." NOT "threaten me again, and you gonna see what happens." My responses were designed to be assertive without escalating tensions or giving my antagonizer anything to latch on to. If I was fouled too hard I would say "FOUL!" realllly loud. If they said, "YOU SOFT, YOU CALLIN BITCH FOULS!" I would act crazy and say, "OH YEAH, WE'RE PLAYIN THE NO-RULES VERSION?!?!? ALLRIGHT, THAT'S THE KIND OF PARTY I LIKE!!!!" That worked every time. That put the image in their heads of some crazy white boy chop-blocking their knees as they went in for a lay-up.

This intolerably long digression aside, I thought would eventually fight this guy named Leeroy. Leeroy was a truly insufferable bully who never had a job or a penny to his name. He was about 5'11" and maybe 190, and just ripped. He stole from people, beat people up, assaulted a friend of mine with a beer bottle, hacked the shit out of me, and cheated in every game. He was also a ball-hog. He destroyed the myth that bullies wouldn't actually fight. I once counted him doing 35 wide-grip pull-ups and I didn't even see him start. Now that you know I was tangling with people like this on the regular, it may give you some insight on why I was interested in taking shit off Cappy and the rest of his ilk.

Leeroy said something pretty funny one day. It was Christmas Day. I didn't go home to Chicago because I was always too poor, and a bunch of us with nothing better to do on Christmas were shooting around. Out of the clear blue sky Leeroy proclaims,

"FUCK Christmas, and FUCK YOU, TOO, PAT!" I actually laughed. I mean, in his mind I suppose I represented the reason for all his bad Christmases. I was the white kid riding the shiny bike around on Christmas Day while the Leeroy family carved a block of government cheese like a turkey. Whatever. I actually was that kid about a trillion years ago. Most of the time, however, Leeroy's shenanigans were anything BUT funny.

Everyone was leery, gun-shy or out-and-out scared of Leeroy, who everyone regarded as a bullying piece of garbage, a community hazard and a major buzzkill. Nobody wanted to stand up to him, no matter how bad he got. Chip explained it thusly, "Would you take your Lamborghini to a demolition derby and go up against a '73 Nova with no hood?" The logic in this was flawless, but Leeroy also knew this and made everyone's life hell.

{A friend tells another funny story of going to the bathroom at the Venice Public Library and there was an apparently-homeless Leeroy giving himself a birdbath in the sink. The guy said when Leeroy looked up, the bathroom instantly transformed itself into a prison cell. Leeroy had that effect on every environment he poisoned.}

Eventually, I made the decision to fight him the next time the chance came up. I had a strategy and everything. I was training pretty seriously for an MMA career that never materialized, so my timing and confidence were as high as they were going to be. I mean, somebody had to take out the trash.

One fine day, he started bullying the hell out of a teammate of mine and I said, "Hey, Leeroy, this isn't the exercise yard of the fucking penitentiary." And I readied myself for action. But the old catfish looked at the lure and went straight to the bottom. He just walked around in a circle growling some nonsense about, "Don't say my name," or something weird and people got in between us. The guy I actually ended up fighting at he hoop court was

106

one of the last people I would have ever expected to fight.

I think Dave was kind of appointed to police my 'tude shortly after I got up on the bleachers one fine day and I made the following community service announcement, "I WANNA LET YOU GUYS KNOW, THE NEXT TIME I GET PUNKED OUT OF MY GAME, IT'S ON, NO QUESTIONS ASKED." I was tired of the endlessly amusing activity called, "Let's Punk Pat Out Of His Game." I planned to slug the next guy who did it and I thought it was sporting to give Fair Warning. My friends thought it was an insane thing for a white guy to say and I'm sure my enemies said amongst each other, "You hear what that white boy said? He is out of his damn mind. Something has got to be done."

[You call a game and pick a team in order of when you show up. If someone shows up after you, their game is after yours, or they can attempt to "punk" you out of yours. I was fed up with being downgraded from player to spectator, all to their amusement.]

I'm assuming a lot of things, but I think a citizen's action committee of sorts appointed or asked Big Dave to do the beatdown. I could be wrong. We just had never had a problem before and we were actually friends who had each other's phone numbers even…

Dave was a big mixed-race guy [6'3", 250] who played drums for some fairly famous bands. He had kind of a clumsy low-post game and wasn't really a tough-talker, but I saw him tell some yoked-up bully off one day. He was well spoken and educated and wore short dreadlocks and glasses. Conscious Brother-type.

A couple days after my infamous announcement, I was guarding Dave in the post and he started crying about how hard I was body-ing him. Ridiculous. First of all, he outweighed me by like 60 pounds and second of all, we were in the damn PAINT. No cryin' in the paint. I told Dave if he wanted to play soft to take his ass out of the key. He told me that he

107

was going to knock me out if I didn't shut up. I just laughed. This was just plain weird. A big guy whining to a smaller guy about physical play? The big guy being Big Dave, who was my friend and also conscious and peaceable, who was now acting all violent. I just laughed it off, which got him madder and he unleashed some really personal insults. Dave, who knew that I was closer to being a broke-ass nigger at that time in my life than a spoiled white boy, started calling me white trash and said something about a trailer park. Well, Dave, sorry you took it to that level because I got racial insults too. I said,

"Hey, Dave, you seem pissed, why don't you go get yourself some OREO cookies, yeah that's what you need to calm down, some OREO cookies." I was guessing that Dave was self-conscious about his kind of white way of talking, and I was correct, sir. He exploded with anger,

"You think that's some funny shit?! You think that's some funny shit?!" And before I knew it, we were fighting.

We kind of started boxing and I was really surprised at how quick Dave's hands were, especially for a big guy. I assumed he would be as clumsy in a fight as he was on the court but he wasn't. We kind of sparred for about forty seconds with nobody getting the advantage. I decided to say "Fuck it" and went all in. I got Dave in a clinch and then grabbed his head. I rocked slightly backward and got him on my hip. I kind of started to judo-style throw him and threw him right on his back. It was funny, I remember this guy Pete saying, "Damn, I never saw Pat do no shit like that, he musta ate his Wheaties today," as I slammed him. Weird thing to hone in on.

Anyway, I slammed him and put my foot right in the middle of his chest and pulled my fist back to fire the coup de grace into his face when SOME GODDAM IDIOT pulls me off. I never got to finish up. I got pulled away, and Dave got up and pretty much went and played basketball for the rest of day undamaged.

Oh well. I hope Dave isn't too embarrassed by this. He's a really good guy. He lost a very close fight to a seasoned and trained opponent.

Funny thing about fighting, in the streets that is, it only matters if you win or lose. In other words, you are going to get made fun of and disrespected or whatever even if you lose a close street fight to Rampage Jackson. It could have been the fight of your life, but people will say, "Man you got your ass kicked." On the other side of the coin, say you sucker punch Haley Joel Osment at Skybar; people will give you way too much credit… whatevs.

CHAPTER SEVENTEEN:
LOSSES AND DRAWs
[ISU FIGHTS AND THE FIGHTING COW]

"You learn more from your losses than your victories" - Too many different fighters to mention

Gentle Reader, I have long delayed writing the chapter of my fighting losses and draws. Yes, these fist-imonious, fist-uculent, fist-abulous and effer-fist-ent tales of Your Author's triumphant, troubling and occasionally completely pointless fistfights has been pointedly lacking in LOSSES AND DRAWS. Oh, sure, there was the long ago tale of the 60-pound Patrick versus Dreaded Erskine, who I portrayed as a veritable third-grade Joe Frazier in the rose-colored 20/20 vision of nostalgia. But have I lost fights as an adult? Have I played Judy to someone else's Punch? Of course, dear friends, and I shall spin their bitter yarn soon enough. Soon enough. Yea, verily. I am stalling here.

I will swallow my ample pride with a cup of this gourmet-assed coffee I am drinking now, scribing away for your entertainment in a Coffee Bean and Tea Leaf in Beverly Hills, CA on The Oldest and Ugliest Laptop in Los Angeles, under the disapproving stares of the staff who have grown weary of Your Scribe nursing a cup of coffee through two, three and even FOUR mandatory two-hour internet wi-fi time-outs, for I am also using my time wisely to chat with babes online!

YET I DIGRESS, hem, haw, drag my feet. Putting pen to these tales of fighting woe is more difficult than putting winter clothing on a recalcitrant child who pretends his body is as flaccid as runny porridge. I have about as much enthusiasm for the retelling and immortalizing of my "L"s and "D"s as I do for watching a Best of Sean Hannity marathon. But sun and the moon have circled the horizons for 44 x 365 days, and I have to tell the tales of the losses and draws. On my birthday, no less! I have lovingly condensed them all into one chapter. Yes, the victories are shot in 35 millimeter Technicolor, the losses on a black and white spycam. The wins get front-page status while the losses share the back page with the Obituaries, Asian massage ads and Reflections… By Sheila Wood.

There was a time when I could proclaim that I hadn't lost a fight in twenty years. Those losses came in 1986, I believe. And that was the year I went 0 and 2 while attending Illinois State.

I have often thought that Illinois white people are tougher than their California counterparts [minorities everywhere are usually toughened by circumstance]. Most people in Illinois come from Chicago, which is a city known for its brawling inhabitants, or from the farmland part of the state, where the people are even tougher. Children are or were taught to settle their differences with a fair fight. This system may have some validity. I have been jumped no less than 5 times outside Illinois and I don't think I ever SAW it happen there.

By 1986, I had sort of flunked out of ASU, and worked at the car wash while my friends were completing degrees from University of Illinois, Boston College, University of Michigan and Eastern Illinois. Grades are important kids.

My girlfriend's father, the saintly Tom Morton, took a day off work and drove me down to Illinois State to make a personal plea to an administrator with the unlikely name of Will Venerable to get my smart but troubled 20-year-old ass back in school because, like others, they feared I would waste my intellect if I didn't stop that downward skid.

Jesus, if they only knew.

Anyway, I got in and obtained student housing and despised just about everything about Illinois State. If Arizona State was Glen Ayre, Illinois State was assuredly Sunset Pool.

Although I loved my acting class, hot acting teacher and the awesome job Will Venerable got me delivering mail, I pretty much hated Illinois State.

112

I remember a friend telling me that after feeding lobster to his cat lobster, it wouldn't touch its usual cat food for a week. That was my reaction to ASU versus ISU… social scene-wise and hot chicks-wise, anyway. The campus was uninspired and unremarkable and it was situated in the middle of Podunk towns and cornfields. The winter wind there made Chicago seem like Barbados.

As far as girls went, for every hot and friendly beauty at ASU, there was a grumpy plain Jane flowing attitude like she was J-LO at ISU. The parties sucked. They consisted of three hundred kids wearing flannel shirts crammed into some students' off-campus frigid and leaky basement where the keg would run out in like twenty seconds. I blundered into one of these parties alone and knowing nobody there, proceeded to get severely drunk. I don't remember what started the fight but I do remember that everyone there was annoyed with me and I think I started some trouble. I got into it with a bearded guy in a brown flannel shirt. I remember he was just laughing at me before, during, and probably after our 'fight', which consisted of him grabbing my head and putting it between his legs in a scissors-lock while he was still standing up until I almost blacked out. Then I was thrown out of the party headfirst into a snow bank like it was an Old West Saloon [and STAY OUT!]. I had abrasions on each cheekbone that lasted about a week.

Later that term, I returned from a party to our dorm floor and found my roommate, Gary, being choked by this jerky guy named Dan. Dan was that rare and dangerous bird: the bully who could actually fight. He was straddled on Gary's chest with his hands around Gary's neck. I immediately jumped to his defense and told Dan if he wanted to mess with someone in dorm room 310 or whatever, he had to go through me first. He got up off of Gary and was more than happy to oblige me. My last fight had been the car wash victory and I was about the same size. Dan was maybe an inch shorter and was probably ten pounds heavier, but we were definitely in the same

113

division. I was very, very drunk but the old adrenaline got flowing and I fought well.

We proceeded to have one of the most awesome fights ever. It was like one of those donnybrooks you would see in an old film about Ireland with the guys slugging it out, breaking chairs over each other's heads, falling into the river, rolling down a hill and scaring away a flock of pigeons. Most street fights last about 30 seconds action-wise, just enough for someone to gain a quick advantage or for the scrap to get bogged down in a stalemate. Dan and I probably sparred through more than 90 seconds of high-octane action. I think it went down like this:

Dan got off of Gary and we squared up. I grabbed Dan and threw him to the floor in what is called a "Head and Arm" throw in wrestling. Jiu-jitsu practitioners have told me that this move is totally garbage, but it was my go-to takedown in wrestling [I was second-string in the Glenbard West freshman 112 lb. Division and only competed in one meet, which I lost] and I practiced it a lot. You grab a guy's head and triceps and throw him over your hip, hopefully onto his head if it is a street scrape, and land on him as hard as you can. [I used this move to dislocate the shoulder of a 245-pound semi-pro football player/ fraternity brother named Spence at ASU in a late night wrestling match; he then supplexed me, and spun my head on the ground like a break-dancer until I had a silver-dollar sized piece of bacon on my forehead for two weeks. He had his arm in a sling for about the same about of time and took his meals in his room in humiliation.]

Anyway, the move worked and I was on top of Dan but I did little to "improve my position" or "ground and pound" as they say in MMA parlance. Dan sort of grabbed a piece of my face or eye or something and used it as leverage to get to his feet. I returned the favor and kind of held him underneath his nose like Moe used to grab Curly from the Three Stooges. We kind of both stood side-by-side holding a portion of each other's face[!] and then separated. We were back to square one and I think I took him down again

114

and we went rolling down the hall as we both threw
both punches and scrambled for a better position. We
fought this way for probably another forty seconds or
so, went around the corner, down another hall, and
somehow returned to where we started, standing face
to face once again. Dan threw two very Erskine-like
left hooks to my temple and I was contemplating
getting the fight back to the floor when the fight
was stopped, I thought prematurely. I had a lot of
juice left in the tank and more tricks up my sleeve,
but that abrupt ending most certainly resulting in a
loss. But it wasn't the end of the fighting that
night.

That night, I had somehow befriended a 6'4" black
guy from the track team and brought him back to the
dorm to do some more drinking with me and Gary. He
watched me lose, broke up the fight and then he
proceeded to kick Dan's ass properly with several
sweeping overhand bitchslaps that left Dan cowering
in a corner. When we asked him why he did that, he
just said, "I couldn't stand that guy."

I never thought of this before, but Dan actually
fought three guys in one night, going 2 and 1,
getting more than his money's worth! Dan behaved
like a complete jag-off, but had acquitted himself
well fight-wise. I asked the track team guy why they
had stopped my fight, a fight that I thought I was
still alive in. He just said, "You weren't doing
enough."

But this loss proved to be useful [to my stupid
fighting 'career'] because it was a long, long, long
time before I lost again. I'm not sure if I really
ever DID lose again, aside from getting jumped.

**FIGHTING TIP NUMBER NINE: Finish Your Fights.
When I had Dan down, I should have laid into him.
When I stopped for a break in the action, feeling we
had fought long enough, Dan cracked me twice hard.**

**FIGHTING TIP NUMBER TEN: TRY NOT TO LOSE. LOSSES
ARE PAINFUL: Looking back, I believe that I fought
hard, skillfully and honorably to lose a close**

fight. But man, did I have to put up with a lot of derision from everyone else in the dorm, culminating in being awarded Dick of The Floor; a horrible and mean-spirited award given out annually to some outcast by a bunch of assholes. Some ugly chick even wrote me a personal note to rub it in.

NOTABLE DRAWS

In the months after I was stabbed, I made a miraculous recovery. I placed 13th out of 300 teams in an annual blind-draw beach volleyball tournament held in Mexico the following summer. I had chronic nerve pain treated by my savior, Yvonne Kriens, acupuncturist.* I got back on my feet financially [well back to a pinky toe as normal, at least] thanks to my mom, Bob Lucey and Howard O'Leary. I was almost as good as new with a horrific scar and a pretty wild story. But, as I mentioned, I thought the fighting skills may have been gone for good. Not that it mattered much. I had been told by every single one of my friends and family to check my anger and shut the fighting down. But I was addicted. I was like that guy smoking a cigarette through his tracheotomy tube. The following fight convinced me that I had lost it and to give up fighting for good. It was Halloween, 2007.

I absolutely LOVE Halloween. I like every single thing about it. Nerds showing hidden personality with wacky costumes, awesome parties, every hot chick in LA dressed like Catwoman, a sexy devil, a dominatrix, a schoolgirl, a harem girl or a sexy cop. We always found cool parties to go to and I usually did pretty well with the girls I met… until they saw my car or my pad.

For the Halloween after my stabbing, I came up with a fantastic and low-maintenance costume that went over HUGE that year. I simply wore a pair of Abercrombie-looking tan shorts, running shoes, a red bandana, a non-working 99-cent store Ipod strapped to my arm, and a pooka shell necklace. I went

116

shirtless. I thought about 20% of the people would get what I was going for, but EVERY person I encountered immediately shouted, "HEY, MATTHEW MCCONAUGHEY!!" Maybe he should switch the look up once in awhile, but then again, it's obviously not broke, so why fix it?

We went to a party in the Hollywood Hills that was stocked with babes, as usual. I was in rare form, but I got way too drunk, albeit in a very happy way. I talked to about twenty different girls and had laughs with all of them. During that period of my life, I was so happy just to be alive, like Ebenezer Scrooge on Christmas day. I actually found someone dressed as Lance Armstrong and, like the real Lance/Matt, palled around with him for awhile. Of course, when you are having a great time like I was having, you are bound to attract a hater or two. By the way, comedian Katt Williams had the greatest take on haters: "Don't get mad at a hater, he's just doin' his job: Hatin'. YOUR job is to make sure if you got ten haters this week, you get TWENTY next week." If I had ten going into the party, I had at least 12 before the night was over.

Well, sitting next to me on a couch was a guy in a cow costume who wasn't having a good time. I didn't notice him because I was chatting up the babe that was on the other side of me. The cow costume was pretty elaborate and expensive-looking. He was sitting there with the cow's head in his lap, sulking. Curiously, he sort of looked like Cappy. He had had enough of "Mathew McConaughey" for an evening. Perhaps he didn't enjoy Matt's poor acting, vain vamping and conceited mugging in the hare-brained Clive Custler adaptation, "Sahara." But then again, nobody did. However, Matt did look very handsome in it, and it was beautifully shot.

"Excuse me." He leaned over to address the girl I was talking to.

"Excuse me, this guy [me!] is an idiot. Aall he is doing is going around and hitting on every girl in here." Wow, guess somebody spiked his punch with

117

Hater-Ade. Being drunk I just regarded him like an ant at a picnic and said something that was about as subtle as what he said, which I believe was, "Why don't you go fuck yourself." Now, this is the wrong approach. When someone says something really, really rude, just MAKE FUN OF THEM. A better response would have been, "Relaaaax. Don't have a cow, man."

FIGHTING TIP NUMBER ELEVEN: AVOIDING A FIGHT BY confronting violence with humor proves you are clever and brave, unflappable and wise.

Instead, I went down to his level and somehow he challenged me to a fight. So People Magazine's sexiest man alive and The Bitter Heifer go out to the driveway and square up. The whole time, a buddy of his who is dressed like Snow White with a 5 O'clock shadow, starts hounding me and threatening me while trying to choke me from behind. Another party guest pulled him off me, and me and The Cow began a half-assed squabble. I was either too drunk or my timing was off, but I was missing badly with my punches. I got him bent over at the waist and was trying to apply a guillotine choke, unsuccessfully, because the large plastic ring that attached the cow's head was protecting his neck. We got separated and I felt the fight was a humiliating draw, proof that my fighting days were best left behind me. For the most part they have been, but the day ain't over yet!

CHAPTER EIGHTEEN:
TOUGH GUY?

"Courtesy is as much the mark of a gentleman as is courage."
-Teddy Roosevelt

By now, or a lot sooner, many of you may be saying, "Who the hell does this guy think he is, some kind of though guy?" That question has quite a few answers.

It's funny, as I sat down at the old Coffee Bean this a.m., all the tables with outlets near them were full and my ancient laptop has a thirty-second battery life. I approached a 25-year-old white kid reading a Norman Mailer [whom someone I vaguely remember called a "fake-ass tough guy"] book. I came up and asked the kid pleasantly if I could share his large table with six chairs. It is a table that is always shared at this location, with good cheer.

The kid gave me a very sullen and half-hearted, "yeah." He had a Ralph's bag on the table that was in my way. After I sat down, he moved it his way. Two centimeters. The kid's a dick. Anger hormones activated by Norman's tales of the naked and the dead? Maybe he aspires to being a Tough Guy, as I once did. Now I just want to be left alone.

For one thing, let me tell you this EXPLICITLY: NEVER EVER confuse being RUDE with being tough. I am going to get into whether I think I am a "Tough Guy" or not in a minute. But if you ARE tough and not a pussy, it allows you the confidence to be polite even when others are being rude. If you have to get into a fight, or want to get into a fight, you had better make damn sure that you are in the right. If you can fight and you are rude; you are not tough. You are a bully. If you are rude and have nothing to back it up with, you are what is popularly known as a punk-ass bitch.

Look, everyone makes mistakes. Everyone has bad days. You might overreact to a friend's perceived sleight, you might get cut off in traffic by someone who just went to the optometrist, you may just have seen that a "book" written by Sarah Palin is on the best-seller list [crayons not included]. But you have to *try* to be patient and polite with people. It's the only way this whole crazy merry-go-round can work.

You know, I have had some of the worst days you can possibly imagine, and I know how to fight. But I have never gone out to a bar with the intention of fighting some stranger. If I am in a dark and violent mood, I stay home. So many guys think that bluff, bluster, threats and aggressiveness make you tough. Those things make you a fucking nuisance, and eventually, if The World is lucky, a nasty chore for the ACTUAL tough guy... that guy who has to waste *his* time and risk *his* butt to rinse you out like a dirty wash rag.

I was once working on a luxury beachfront house in Malibu. A man came in to look at the house to rent it and I had to show him how to get around the house. Then I returned to work. He graciously introduced himself and his lovely and friendly wife. When he left, he came back and thanked me personally and the migrant workers for their courtesy. His wife came all the way to the back room we were painting and gave a little wave. The man's name was Carlos Norris. As a child, he was teased all the time for his half-Mexican heritage, so he learned karate. He became world Karate champion in 1966, 67, 68, 69, etc., went to Hollywood and the rest is history. One of the toughest guys ever, period. One of the classiest men I have ever met. If he can be nice, so can you. You know him by his nickname, Chuck. Chuck Norris. I did not make a word of that up.

I go to basketball courts all the time and there is this attitude of some kids of the younger generation to talk shit and act all "ghetto." It seems that they have learned everything about being a man from playing Grand Theft Auto. Or from these ridiculous fake-ass gangsters they see on MTV. Gangsters. Gangstas. Whatever.

Gangs are multi-level drug and prostitution marketing scams where the guys at the top get very rich and the rest of the guys stay poor, get killed, or go to prison, and not for just 45 days like your Humble Scribe. The guys at the top get homeless people, crack whores or dumb kids with no opportunities to carry the drugs they never touch. They are some of the cruelest and most miserable people on earth. They buy and sell human lives for little vials of crack. When in a gang, you have to do everything the guy above you tells you to do; whether it is beating up a righteous man, getting shot to death or sucking somebody's dick. Gangs are a perfect refuge for sadistic cowards. You don't have to fight your own battles like a man with your fists; you can get your "boys" or "your gat." The former gangsters you see on MTV or in the movies have a curious dilemma: Once they get rich, they can become "punk-ass sell-outs," wisely leaving gang life behind and calling the police every time another black person walks across their front lawn in their new, mostly-white neighborhood. Or they can "keep it real" by staying gangsters, keep their gang ties, and get murdered when they finally have something to lose (or visit Las Vegas). [You want to get rid of gangs? Legalize drugs and prostitution.]

But nowadays **everyone** wants to be a gangster. I see kids with their pants half off their asses, acting like the SHIT is about to POP OFF with STEEL IN THEIR EYES... whilst carrying Crate and Barrel bags at the posh Beverly Center mall. I've seen Armenian teenagers screaming to their colleagues, "YOU DON'T KNOW ME, NIGGA, WASSUP NIGGA!!" It's the hip-hop culture, the gangster ways that have perpetuated so much rudeness, pointless violence, idiocy, misogyny and truly unfortunate fashion victims.

Am I a tough guy? I don't know, but I like to think, at least at certain times in my life, I could take a rude, tough-talking, bullying imposter and give him a real Ambush Makeover. There was a time where I would stand listening to a Tough Guy Threatening Resume [you don't know me cuz; don't know where I'm from; don't you know I'm loco] [sigh], like a dog licking its chops, waiting for a kid's ice cream to fall off the cone. But not anymore. I've done my part. It's time for some others to take up the torch.

Do I think I am a tough guy? I would be THE VERY FIRST person to ring the bell to quit in Navy Seal training, probably on the bus ride to the first challenge. I would last three seconds in the part where they sit in the cold surf. I even hate it when that cold spray hits you from your shower head in the morning. I would last maybe twenty seconds, if I were running, with a top boxer or cagefighter. I have met dozens of ordinary citizens, friends, cops, bouncers and construction workers that would likely kick my ass but it would never get to that because they are TOUGH, they know the code, and they would never tangle with another righteous man over something trivial.

I am not tough enough to work in a factory, coal mine or grocery store for 50 hours a week, and patiently provide for a wife and children. I would get killed or crippled instantly in an NFL football game. I cut a cyst off my head once and I thought that was pretty tough until I saw the guy on Dateline who sawed his own arm off with a **Swiss Army knife** to get out from under a boulder. Am I as tough as the severely handicapped girl with a deformed ribcage that smiles at you every time you walk into Baja Fresh, even though she is working circles around everyone there? Not bloody likely.

Am I as tough as that little Chinese guy who squared up on the tank in Tiananmen Square? [Nobody knows his name, but I am pretty sure he is still in a cell without a Sleep Number Bed.]

As a child, I desperately wanted to be a tough guy. Probably because I was aware of the fact that I was growing up a Sheltered Pussy, a couple school fights aside. I wanted to be tough like the guys in the movies, I'll give you an example:

My friend Craig Samborski had a sleepover birthday party at his dad's apartment. [Toughness aside, a good example of how OBNOXIOUS I was, when his avuncular dad introduced himself to us 3rd grade kids as "Myron but you can call me Mike," I said, "Nah, I think I'm gonna call you Myron."] Craig's uncle, some old-school old-country Polish character asked if any of us kids wanted a shot of whisky and actually poured some in a shot glass. Tim Bixler, Rob Matthews and Doug Wilkins all tried to taste it, recoiling as soon as the shot glass touched their lips. I called them pussies and grabbed the thing like John Wayne and gave it the old heave-ho, down the hatch. I woke up 1 second later on my back with the stuff spraying out of my nose.

I started drinking coffee as a teenager. I took pride in the fact that my dad put a half-teaspoon of sugar in his, while I, like a tough guy, took mine black. I now drink my coffee with a half of a packet of cocoa mix, preferably the type with mini-marshmallows.

I desperately wanted to box, but I had to take like three commuter trains out of my neighborhood to find a place that actually taught it. I was something of a prodigy and I was sparring full speed with the instructors, but my career was sidetracked by laziness and a lack of dedication to disciplined training beyond spirited shadow-boxing to "Take On Me." The real tough guys couldn't stand me at the gym. I was a talented kid who had range, a fast and stiff jab, a good right and the humility of Saddam Hussein. They used to take cheap shots at me out of the clinch or at the bell, which I took as a compliment. They sure as hell weren't giving these 'extra lessons' to the other students. Bob Beals was always castigating the instructors for their treatment of me. But they knew, and I knew, with a smirk, if they didn't beat me down, I would time them, range them and embarrass them. I loved the fact that they actually had to fight me and I took my extra lumps stoically. They were, in fact, gold stars. I never got the chance to thank the guys.

TOUGHER ERA?

I grew up in the 70s, when we had far superior species of Tough Guy Celebrity Role Models than the kids of today, aside from some athletes of today who are tougher than hell. Some of the movies stars that played tough guys actually were tough guys! Steve McQueen, who did his own car stunts and stole a tank off a Marine base, Charles Bronson allegedly grew up so poor that he had to wear his sister's hand-me-down dresses to school. Kirk Douglass, whose Dickensian childhood was ridiculously tough, got to play Spartacus, the toughest man in history. You wouldn't catch any of them hopping up and down on Oprah's couch like a first grade girl after eating a movie-sized box of Red Hots. We also had Muhammad Ali who was simultaneously the greatest boxer and the funniest man on FREE television. Even guys like Paul Newman and Robert Redford, while not street squabblers, showed amazing toughness, integrity and character throughout their lives on and off screen.

And then there was Evel Kneival, a guy whose toughness was definitely beyond psychotic. [Evel's life exploits were the subject of some of the greatest and most-spirited discussions in grade school history. There have been very few debates I have found as interesting in my life as our vociferous lunch room arguments as to the length of Evel's upcoming record jump, how many bones he had broken in the last one, or how Evel could have broken 354 bones when a simple glance at The Encyclopedia Britannica would show the human body only contained 273… "but, duuuude, he broke a lot of those bones TWICE (all evidence was anecdotal as there was no internet)] I have often mused that there is nobody in the world who has been a dealt a worse hand than Robbie Kneival, whose inheritance was not a bakery, a savings and loan or woodworking shop, but an obligation to jump over busses on a motorcycle.

In this book, I write about fistfights. It is difficult to say how many of them I regret, how many of them I could have solved a better way, and which

124

ones I was glad I did what I did. It's funny and maybe moot to try to think of all the environmental causes for my fighting. Maybe I was just born to fistfight. God's will. *to you believe this*

God. OK, I believe in God, big-time. Jesus, to be exact. Not spiritualists that sell food steamers, not Agape, not Allah, not Buddha, L. Ron Hubbard or Shiva, although I almost NEVER talk about it. I believe it was God's plan for me to end up where I am and take the journey that I have taken.

As a smart-ass and cynical child, I was an atheist. Yet, I was an excellent literary critic with a nose for bullshit. I finally read the New Testament, and I didn't find any BS in there… none at all. Pretty far from it. ['Cept for that part where Jesus turns the other cheek, it would have been nice if He had kicked some Roman ass, but that's just my insane take.] Who am I to second-guess The Lord?

I don't want to fight in the streets anymore. I want to fight to free child slaves and liberate victims from the torturous prisons of Syria, North Korea and Arizona. I want to fight to show people that the Greatest Charade In History is the New Electric Car. Chevron owns the old one, the perfectly good one. They just don't want you to have it, and all it's maintenance-free glory. It sits on a shelf in a warehouse like the Ark discovered by Indiana Jones.

I want to fight to show the good people of this country that corporate influence and ownership of most TV and radio outlets has truly run amok to the point of giving us the most disastrous energy policy on earth, the worst two-term U.S. president in history, senators that deny climate change, a banking system that extorts and blackmails the U.S. public, and a U.S. senate that just declared that corporations have all the rights of citizens. Misinformation mismanaged for the benefit of the mighty few. [Fox "News" may be the clearest symptom that the end is near and I believe that every employee there will burn in everlasting hell…]

125

I forget where I was going with all of this. But one thing you can be sure of: I am a fighter.

Do I think I am some kind of tough guy? Would it surprise you that after my first confrontation with BILLY, WARRIOR PRINCESS, I was tired of the feud, came to my senses and feared for my safety? Would you be shocked to know I saw a man slap a girl in the face *hard* in Manhattan Beach and did absolutely nothing about it, because I was too high... and scared. I have a pretty long list of these, actually. I am sure you have your own list. I think maybe only *true cowards* do not have a list of cowardly acts that weigh on their soul. {Bartlett's, you taking this down? mm, yes?}

I have integrity. I am an honest man. I try to stick up for others and what I know is right. I try to be fair. I have worked patiently and sacrificed financial success for artistic integrity. I have fought physically not just for myself but on the behalf of others. I have treated others less fortunate than me with compassion.

But, I certainly would NEVER call myself a tough guy and I think it is a dangerous folly to think of myself that way. But I have to remind myself of this fact. I was not born with an over-active Humility Gland, Gentle Reader.

I have found that proclaiming that you are tough guy is a sure way of finding yourself an emporer without any clothes, and this is a lesson I am likely not finished learning.

CHAPTER NINETEEN:
COUPLE NOTES ON VENICE BEACH, 2000-2006:
'IN THE CREASE'

[Various Venice Beach fights condensed, Baja Cantina I and II, Rick I and II]

"Happy people don't cause much trouble."
-Patrick Davis

I suppose the years I lived in Venice Beach were the most violent times of my life. I optioned a screenplay in 1999, made ten grand, got out of the Hollywood Motel Hell and went 180 degrees to an amazing lifestyle. I rented a large boat in Marina Del Rey to live aboard and assumed that fame and fortune were right around the corner. There were a lot of things around the corner but fame and fortune were certainly not two of them.

I was trying to woo a girl I was desperately in love with, which ended in a world-class disaster. The option money ran out, yet I fell back asswards into another great situation: my neighbor in the slip next to mine, Jim Duggan, owned a corporate jet company and moved off his even larger and more luxurious yacht. Jimmy befriended me and hired me to learn the business, perhaps become a pilot, be a gopher and wash airplanes [after working at a car wash and washing 60-foot-long aircraft, I can bucket wash a car in about 90 seconds]. He thought I might make it as a pilot because of this insane car stunt I used to pull on a regular basis to relieve stress and boredom. I won't elaborate because I don't want kids trying it at home.

For various reasons I won't get into, my luck ran out there and, by 2002, I was writing some for NOBODY, living on a tiny sailboat that had the interior room of a SUV, and was scrambling for any kind of work without a real trade, sometimes even scraping the paint off boats for $8 an hour. I was marina trailer trash. I eventually learned to be a carpenter by working like a slave for some of the biggest assholes on planet earth, optioned my screenplay again to two of the biggest scumbags on earth, and rented a shared bedroom from one of the biggest dickwads on earth.

I think my truly horrible luck began to end in 2003 when I began to be a mildly prosperous carpenter who spent a lot of time at the beach and bars. I probably only had a car half the time. I was always, according to one girlfriend, "a heavy drinker that was bad with money."

I had some great roommates, some bad roommates and some truly monstrous roommates. A poor man, like Marilyn Monroe, is a candle in the wind. These Venice years were a real roller coaster ride. I'm sure that many people considered me weird or simply insane.

I had manyfriends from the two sports I played, and a lot of very short-term girlfriends, but the period between 2002 and 2005 was very turbulent, poverty-stricken, beer-soaked, depressing and violent. You could say that I was a little reckless during that period. There were days I wouldn't wear my favorite summer footwear, flip-flops, because there was a decent chance I would get into a scrap and need better squabbling traction. There were days that I packed warmer clothes in my car in case I were to be arrested for a dust-up, which is very smart as anyone who has ever been booked into freezing cold jail wearing only swim trunks will tell you [experience talking here]. I have to temper my tales of woe with the fact that I have always done well meeting women, and some of these brief affairs and one-night stands with the ubiquitous LA beauties really were all I had going on. Thanks, ladies.

I am not a big hockey fan, but I have a friend named Noel who is. I was describing my feud with BILLY, WARRIOR PRINCESS and he said, "So when you get around Abbot's Habit coffee shop, you are in the

128

crease." He explained that in the sport of hockey, the area around the goal is the most heavily fortified and violently defended. It's called "the crease." You just don't skate through the crease willy-nilly, you better have your ass bunched up and your head on a swivel. Well, that's kind of how those years went. I already detailed the fights with Cappy and Dave the Drummer from the Venice years. I guess I can go into some of the other notable squabbles of the era which would be: Baja Cantina, I and II, Rick Cheswick I and II, and The Brig part II.

THE BATTLES FOR BAJA

The Baja Cantina fights were fairly simple affairs. One wasn't even really a fight. Although the Baja it is still one of the several Los Angeles bars that I have been Banned For Life from.

The Baja Cantina is an all-time great bar. It's 2 blocks from the Venice Beach Pier, it's big and casual, the drinks are reasonably-priced, the staff is great, the bartenders tell jokes, the girls working there are hot, and the babes were running like grunion from the years 2000 through 2004. My beach volleyball buddies used to go there after playing several games every weekend. OK, my life wasn't always THAT bad. No matter how broke I was, I could scrounge up 9 bucks: 4 for the pre-drink, a pint of paint-removing vodka to get into character, then 4 bucks for a nursed draft beer, with a buck left over for a tip. Look, it's a system. I never bought girls a drink. [One of the few times I did: the girl, upon receiving said cocktail, promptly and smugly told me that she had a boyfriend. I swear to God that I just looked her in the eye, stuck a straw into her drink, drained it and walked away. Gold diggers move along… sugardaddy I ain't.]

One afternoon, I was talking to a beautiful girl, who was politely suspending disbelief and good sense like you have to in order to enjoy an "Ernest Goes To" movie, when a group of noisy and obnoxious drunks at the next table interrupts us to challenge me to an arm-wrestling match with one of their boys. I now know the proper response to this, which is, "Sorry guys, I'm not gay." I don't know what the hell got into me, but I like to arm-wrestle, so I did it. I won and then took my new friend to a different part of the bar when the guys began leering at her and making stupid comments. Fight-avoiding ninja strikes again! Not so fast.

Fast forward a couple hours and I am near the entrance. The girl, having come to her senses or having been "rescued" by her friends, has flown the coop. I am amicably swapping jokes with Big Mike, the bartender.

The arm-wrestling dorks are now being bum-rushed out the door by the security staff. Apparently, they were bugging EVERYONE. One of the guys comes up on me, pure madness in his eyes and pokes me in the chest, his voice a strangled rasp, his face beet-red: "THIS **ASSHOLE** IS THE REASON, THE REEEEEASSSSON WE'RE GETTING KICKED OUT!!!"

FIGHTING TIP NUMBER TWELVE: Do your threatening and shit-talking from a distance no closer than 38 inches, under no circumstance touch a person you are threatening or talking shit to.

Gentle Reader, when Fight-Avoiding Ninja makes his first appearance, many fools drunk on the wine of their own bluster, mistake him for a pussy, a coward, a pacifist or someone who will fight under no circumstances.

Sometimes this Angel of Mercy appears for your protection, not his. Fight-Avoiding Ninja, does not, like Gandhi, Jesus or the current Mrs. Tom Cruise, have an infinite reservoir of shit-taking memory space in his hard drive.

I don't know, I looked at him coolly for about a half second and then when I realized there was some physical exclamation point on its way, I exploded into action. I grabbed his head and slammed it into a wall in the narrow hallway, then I slammed his head into the bar on the other side, then I slammed his head onto the wall again, then I slammed his head onto the floor, where I punched him in the face very hard twice. Bodies flew, people screamed and bystanders were injured.

I was stormed by the bouncers and I wriggled out of their grasp and absconded out the back door as fast as my little legs could carry me, thus completing the CRITICAL and more important second leg of the bar fight biathlon: The escape. Beat up and BEAT FEET. As the great tight end-turned-commentator, Shannon Sharpe, said of an NFL player who lingered around a squabbling pile-up too long only to be injured by a cheap shot, "Stay away from that pile, no need to look at that pile, nothin' good happenin in that pile." It's the same with the post-melee atmosphere of the street fight victory. The wine of an al fresco pugilism victory is best enjoyed in front of a roaring fireplace, trusty dog at your feet, and a little George Michael "Careless Whisper" on the old phonograph to dial the temper down. *In short, get out of there, go home!*

Nobody is going to bring you a ribbon, a hot girl or even a Cup O'Noodles. Al Michaels will not ask you if you are going to Disneyland. Ed McMahon will not magically appear with a chuckle and an over-sized check. The police will be there soon enough and your victim might come back with his boys or a weapon. Nothing worth hanging around for.

I was banned from Baja for a period of one year. I did my time standing on my head, hey, there's more than one bar in LA.

I guess some years later I was standing in exactly the same spot at Baja when I received a violent shove in the back. I turned to see an old codger who looked a bit like Kenny Rogers, and he dropped into a fighting stance. I had never seen him in my life. He didn't look too formidable so I palmed his face like a basketball and put it on the bar. It had a calming effect on him.

Rick Cheswick is a good friend and hilarious guy that kind of looked like an adult version of Bam-Bam from "The Flintsones," but he wasn't buffed. Rick would get severely drunk and start fistfights with people who also had a kind of cartoonish quality. He even got Oscar De La Hoya to take a swing at him in a Mexican nightclub once. We always hung out on my boat before Jim repo'd it and we had a terrible band called NBG [Nothin But Gold], with Rick on keyboards, me on vocals, with Diesel Derek on guitar and spoken word. Diesel Derek was an absolute genius of the Michigan J. Frog variety, who would say the funniest things ever and then clam up or forget them the instant we got tape rolling.

We went to a very posh party at this computer genius software designing think-tank house in the Venice Canals. This guy Billy was running the house that attracted all these top eggheads to design voice-activation software. To get all the eggheads to stay, he made the place really fun to live at and there were always great parties there.

Billy was trying to be Bill Gates meets Hugh Hefner and doing a pretty decent job of it.

NBG rolled to the party in full effect and we started having a great time. Rick was harboring a grudge at me for "fucking up his ride." I had somehow damaged his badass vintage Benz by going into a driveway too fast when I was designated driver, God knew how drunk the other guys were for *me to be driving*... and I had no ability to pay to fix it. My leg was also in the second-hand skeevy leg brace that a client gave me and I really couldn't work. Rick was always mellow, but he let things stew and had Bad Episodes every now and then. He was in one of his moods that night. I think he pushed Diesel Derek into the water earlier in the evening, ruining his phone and leather coat, which Rick thought was the funniest thing in the history of comedy. Derek was about 6'3" and 220 but didn't have a fighting bone in his body, but he was almost ready to swing on Rick.

We had dried Diesel D. off and calmed him down before we hit the party. But Rick kept on laughing about it and Derek was still pissed. I thought I had better keep an eye on them. I didn't want to see them fight.

I was kind of on a roll with the girls that week and while I was talking to a pretty one Rick came up to us and said to her, "Hey, there is no way you are gonna sleep with this guy, I won't allow it." Can you believe that? I tried to calm him down without spoiling the atmosphere I had been creating, saying quietly, "Hey, Rick, you can't talk to people that way."

Rick informed me that he was going to talk to me any way he wanted and I just tried to ignore him. Rick had a plastic Super Big Gulp cup full of a frozen margarita, one of those friggin pails that holds like 64 ounces. He just looked at me and upended the damn thing on my head. He then ran down the hall and tried to lock himself in the bathroom. I hopped all the way and got to the door just as he was slamming it. I busted in and threw him on the ground and tried to slam his head on the floor hard, sensing I was probably going to re-blow out the delicate knee, which was not really supported by this bootleg knee brace that looked like it had been some soldier's brace in the Civil War. [I have been telling stories to my buddies about this time period while writing the book and they both remarked about how horrible that thing looked]

We were thrown out of the party, which pissed me off even more than the fight because this guy Billy was cool and the type of person that I needed to be friends with. He seemed to have it more together than the members of NBG at the very least. Now Billy thought we were a couple of idiots, Beavis and Butthead, turds in the punchbowl, hoi polloi... especially in comparison to a shwanky crowd of computer geniuses. So me and Rick are standing outside the door, he's got his head downcast like he is ashamed and I said, "What the hell?"

Rick was playing possum. All of a sudden he picks up this skateboard that someone has left outside and swings it at my head. Here we go again.

This time, I'm even angrier and even more worried about my knee, so I got Medieval with his ass. I dodged the skateboard, which went right past my face, and I grabbed him by his shoulders and spun him to the ground, all the while hopping on one leg. It wasn't that hard, Rick was like five sheets to the wind. I then proceeded to grate the side of his head like a block of aged Parmesan on the wrought-iron fence until he stopped struggling. When we left him there, he was conscious but extremely fucked up and bleeding. Diesel and me had had enough of his capers for one evening, but we weren't that worried about his health. Rick was exceptionally durable. I remember he would go body-surfing drunk in the shore break at Malibu until his back was covered with road rash from getting slammed on the rocks and he'd just come up laughing.

Me and Derek and a few others returned to my boat for one of our terrible jam sessions that were very reminiscent of the band from "Slingblade." You'll never guess who shows up. **It's Rick,** get this, with blood running down the side of his face and plastered in his hair. He is also wearing a cop's motorcycle helmet that he claims he needs for protection from me. It was so funny that we let him onto the boat and we proceeded to have a jam session without further incident.

We were clearly the types of savages better off with our own company than that of polite society.

BRIG PART TWO

It is actually Part One, because it precedes the Cappy fight, obviously, because after that one I was BFE from The Brig [Banned For Eternity.]

134

I was standing at the bar, waiting for a drink that would never come per usual, when I see and hear something completely odd. There is a guy in a black dress shirt *cursing out* a couple of girls. He is pretty big and he has an English accent. It went something like:

"NO, YOU watch where YOU'RE GOING or I'll shove you again, I've got plenty more where that came from!" The two girls looked at the guy in horror. This was Beyond The Pale even by L.A. Idiot Community Standards. "Plenty more where that came from?" [Too bad there wasn't an L.A. TV producer nearby, they would have given him his own series: The Rudest Guy Ever Show. Chicks from all over the country would audition to have drinks spilled on them, bartering their dignity as human beings for ten seconds of air time for Even Stupider People to watch and discuss; the basic premise of all reality shows.]

I know the right move for this type of situation now. It's simple. Pay attention. *You go get the security staff and tell them there is some drunk threatening women at the bar.* A nice premium beer costs one dollar at the store. It costs seven dollars at The Brig. Part of that surcharge is that they, like every other bar, are obligated to provide you a safe environment to enjoy your cocktail. It is widely known that alcohol acts as a catalyst for the acting-out enzyme in the primitive flatworm-sized brain of guys with issues. Those who work in the nightclub business are aware of this. I have become such a valued spotter for security in bars I go to. Like a secret agent. Curtis, who is 6'5" and 300 pounds had a great technique when I told him about someone acting creepy. He would just go stand four inches behind the guy. They generally calmed down fast.

I just kind of snapped in this case. I looked at the guy after I got my beer [by some miracle]. I held the glass out from by body and turned into him with my stiffened forearm, knocking him sideways. He

135

was like, "What the hell," and I told him that I had plenty more where that came from.

At first he kind of protested and asked what I was doing messing with him and that his deal with the girls was his business… and then he kind of changed gears all of a sudden and challenged me to a fight outside. I was slightly worried because they guy had all this scary scar tissue around his eyes. However, it probably meant he was prone to **losing** fights.

The fight was pretty uneventful, for me anyway. I remember it was over very fast with the guy on his back getting punched and me getting dragged off him. I used the same formula as I did to win many fights. A very fast jab and straight right, opponent rushes you in a panic, use his momentum to take him past you, trip him, take him down. Garnish with knuckle samwidges. Lather, rinse and repeat as necessary. Disappear.

I was allowed back in the bar and he was tossed. The security staff knew I never went looking for trouble.

They even knew that the Cappy thing wasn't my fault, but I was banned anyway. I understood their logic; I mean, **you sell** the lawn mower that chopped all dad's fingers off, even though it was his damn fault for reaching under it while it was running.

Once inside, I saw a guy I hadn't seen in years, all the way back from Hawaii times, and I tell him what happened. He tells me that I just kicked his friend's ass and how I had gotten lucky because he was some Badass Legendary Soccer Barbrawling Hooligan or something. Lucky, huh? Funny, I didn't see any dice or cards out there. He may have simply created his own legend, I mean, how are you going to fact-check something like that?

CHAPTER TWENTY:
MUSIC APPRECIATION DAY

In 1986 Chicago, I used to take a commuter train to my boxing gym. A little post Car Wash era. I brought my guitar along occasionally. I didn't look like much. Very skinny, like I said before. I was returning from practice one afternoon. It was cold and snowy so it must have been one of the ten and a half winter months of Chicago

I took the guitar out of the case and this beefy, 50-year-old construction worker guy yells, "Hey, buddy, no way, not happening." He was like ten seats away. I had no intention of playing it loudly like a street performer. I think I was getting it out of the case just to tune the strings out of raging boredom. I looked at him and started playing it, soft as hell, just to annoy him. At the time I couldn't play guitar to save my life, but I didn't like this guy's position on The Humanities or how he chose to educate me on it. One sure way to get me to do something is to tell me **not to** do it in a very rude fashion. But I did not want to annoy the other passengers, just *him.*

The conductor walked by and I asked him if it was OK if I played at a quiet level. The conductor said, "Sure, of course." I smirked at construction dude. Laws on **my side**, pops. [When I was a kid, the neighbor's house was getting demolished. The firemen used to set practice fires in it before it was actually torn down. I used to hang out and talk to them from the other side of the fence. What kid wouldn't want to watch firemen set practice fires all day? On their last day, I asked them if I could throw rocks through *all* the windows when they left. The firemen laughed and told me, "Sure." I gathered a huge pile of stones and didn't even tell my friends. I was going to hog this magical experience and savor it like a fine cognac. The funnest part wasn't throwing rocks through the windows, which was *fun as hell.* The best part was when grown-ups stopped to yell at me and I politely told them to fuck off and that I had **permission** from the *fire department* and they were *more than welcome* to check that.]

Construction guy, whose act is a little reminiscent of Archie Bunker's [he actually *looked more* like Jimmy The Greek in a red flannel], too old to be causing trouble at any rate, has *had it.* He gets up and walks up to my seat with a big buddy in tow. They approach my seat and he says, with complete confidence:

"You better put that guitar way, sonny." I had an answer for that, which was the last thing they expected to hear from a skinny nerd guitar-playing vagabond dude.

"**You** better sit your fat ass down before I kick it."

Gentle Reader, the look on his face was *priceless.* It was as if he thought he was going to kick a sand castle only to find it was built around a cinder block.

He kind of half-turned away, wondering how he had possibly miscalculated this Gimme of a Manly Moment. His large buddy, who was somewhere around my age, and wearing a cloth military jacket, reached past him and grabbed my collar. Zounds! Lancelot to his corpulent, art-hating and buttinsky Guinevere! The champion of guitar-hatin' Archie Bunker-types.

I stood and Archie Bunker didn't do much but his beer belly stopped me from maneuvering very well in the confined area. Lancelot took the opportunity to reach past him and lay three right hooks to my jaw. I have always had a good chin and, despite his size, home-boy didn't hit very hard. I just looked him right in the eye as he did it.

The fight was broken up, and the Only Black Guy in Chicago's Western Suburbs came up to my seat to tell me he had my back. You just can't write this shit but I guess I am. The rest of the passengers on the train voiced their anger and shook their heads in disgust at how uncalled for and cowardly the attack had been. The two Tough Construction Workers returned to their seats to glower and I had made up my mind that wherever they got off, I was getting off too, we had some business to finish. I was **pissed.**

Archie Bunker got off before Lancelot. Given the choice between him and Lance, I chose Lance. Archie Bunker looked pretty terrified while Lance was still actively mad-dogging me. Luckily, Lancelot got off at my stop. I pointed to him and myself and to a spot in the parking lot, like "you and me, right now." Maybe twenty people, mostly office-types in suits, gathered in a circle on that cold winter day to see what the hell was going to happen next. It's just a simple truth, everyone **loves** watching a fight.

Lance, who is probably around 6"1" and 200, going bald very early and looking a little bit like a beefier version of Dwight from "The Office." He was way, way bigger than I was. BUT, I was boxing every day against pro fighters, hitting the heavy bag until my shoulders were about to drop off and I thoroughly believed that, despite my having zero pro or amateur fights, the current 1986 middleweight champion, Thomas "The Hitman" Hearns would be looking at me nervously through his rearview mirror soon enough. But I definitely needed to get through this tool first if I were to ever have my chance at The Motor City Cobra, who had recently and foolishly moved up from 154 to My Division: 160. [Due to the fact I never derailed him, The Hitman won belts at 147, 154, 168 and 175, but he's never thanked me]

I had these really cool red suede Puma track shoes that I had bought, but they were kind of slippery because they had removable cleats which I had already removed... this led me to realize perhaps the Most Important Street Fight Rule of All:

FIGHTING TIP NUMBER THIRTEEN: Be Aware of Terrain, Especially Footing. [I can't tell you *how many fights* I have seen lost by someone slipping. Half of all jail fights turn when one combatant slips on a Dorito bag. Street fights are very nervous affairs, so a lot of guys over-commit to a big punch, and windmill right past their opponent and onto the ground. Jiu-jitsu practitioners are taught to fight well off their backs, yet I have never seen anyone gain advantage from that position in any of the maybe sixty or seventy street fights I have seen/ been in. But you better watch your ASS if you start any shit in Brazil. I have also used nearby objects as cudgels to slam people into and low-laying objects to push people over.]

I set down my guitar, and Lance got the festivities rolling by walking over and kicking it. Dude. It was a little "on the nose."

He looked very nervous. I was desperately trying to keep my cool and not panic. All I had to do was throw like I threw every day at the Gym and this fight *should* be a Teddy Bear Picnic for me. But there was ice *everywhere* in the parking lot of the Glen Ellyn Train Station and I had slippery shoes on. I kind of subtly maneuvered over to a place where I could stand on a dry hole in the ice-covered parking. Homeboy's spot, as he squared up across from me, looked to be a little icy. Oh well.

He got his fists up and I bounced a little for balance and threw a very rapid, accurate and hard 1,1,2 combo: Jab, jab, right. They all hit him square in the face and he scrambled on the ice like the Three Stooges. He rushed me and I got his cloth army jacket with both hands like he was wearing a Karate Gi and wheeled him to the icy ground where I began plying rights into his face and slamming his head into an ice lump for good measure until the crowd pulled me off.

He was battered and bleeding, but I'm sure otherwise fine. He walked away under his own power.

140

I wasn't big [or mean and crazy] enough yet to lay down the severely psychotic beating I put on The Circle Bar Douche. But there is something *just horrible* about losing a fight on a winter day. I remember teasing this fat kid named Craig Russell in Junior High until he charged me like rhinoceros and stuffed my head in a snow bank until I almost blacked out. Crying, losing and clearing ice and snow out of your eyes, ass and especially ears is a DRAG.

CHAPTER TWENTY-ONE:
KARAOKE BAR FIGHT

"Karaoke is the combination of people who shouldn't be singing with people who shouldn't be drinking" - anon

So Sandy and I are working at the nicest karaoke bar in Southern California, the name will come to me. Yama Teppan. Got it on the rewrite. It's not that catchy.

Karaoke was a relatively new thing in 1993 and the job was kind of a hoot. I got it out of the Want Ads because I actually did the job in Hawaii and I'm good in an interview as well as on a microphone. Sandy had made me eat these terrible frozen burritos UNTIL I GOT A JOB. She bought a box of 3000 of them for twelve bucks at Costco. That was breakfast, lunch and dinner for me until I got a job. I looked hard.

This place was PLUSH. It was a Japanese restaurant, sushi bar and karaoke lounge. The LOUNGE had the best sound system ever and the staff was a blast to hang out with… Sandy was trying to rehabilitate me from the guy who showed up at her house from Hawaii with his possessions literally in a grocery bag [toothbrush, two pairs of shorts and a t-shirt]. We had to tell everyone she knew that they had lost my luggage. Sandy rolled up her sleeves and tried to make some lemonade out of this lemon but it never really worked. We had some great times anyway.

I was a very sarcastic DJ on the mike, but I also liked some of the singing. As the best of its kind, our karaoke bar attracted some actual world-class singers, and some world-class losers who would sing the same retarded song night after night. I learned a trick. If I had gotten really weary of a song, I told the patron that the track they wanted was on a laser disc that was broken. It was funny, people would get chappy as hell over that stupid shit. One time when I wasn't there, there was a giant free-for-all brawl where some chick lost a tooth.

One night, after working there for some time, I went up to the bar and ordered a drink. Sandy was forcing me to cut down on my drinking and she only allowed me to have one per night. My friend Dan, the bartender, pretended to make it a big foo-foo drink but it was actually like 20 ounces of vodka with a teaspoon of something to make it a different color. The staff would have been really fun people to party with if Sandy had ever let me. She was many things, but stupid wasn't one of them.

This odd, buffed and aggressive guy bumped the hell out of me while I was getting my drink from the bar. I just said "excuse me" and guarded that drink like a short-yardage fullback protecting a football with a slim late fourth-quarter lead.

I returned to the bar later during a long song, maybe the hated "Like a Rolling Stone" with its 28 depressing and, in my opinion, sucky verses. I liked to rap with Dan who the took most critical part of bartending, telling jokes, seriously. The guy who bumped me is still at the bar, like six chairs down. He called out:

"Hey, buddy, you gotta watch where you are GOING."

I had forgotten him but now remembered. I was in a great headspace. I was among friends and getting buzzed as hell on my secretly spiked drink. The guy was just a miserable prick, he should get a dog or something. I just was like:

"Oh, yeah, man, sorry bout that."

He kept looking at me with his weird big eyes, mad-doggin' me. He said:

"YEAH, YOU NEED TO WATCH WHERE YOU ARE GOING!"

144

Something woke up inside me. My little bubble [sex with a beautiful woman every day, an easy job, people that liked me, the warm California sun] kinda popped. I replied without thinking:

"HEY, DUDE, GUESS WHAT? I TAKE IT BACK. I'M NOT SORRY ANYMORE. AT ALL."

He strode up to me and shoved me with two hands in my chest. Just like that. Dollar signs had rung in *his* eyes. He wanted a fight and now he found someone dumb enough to take him up. A soft-looking white boy, to boot, booyah. Dude looked crazy.

After the fight, my buddy Jeff told me that this guy was a crazy and violent badass and had just gotten out of prison [he obviously missed it]. Jeff had heard about our fight through the grapevine and that the guy, with the odd name of Kanzu, was now looking for me and was planning to kill me. Why was he planning to kill me, Gentle Reader? Well, he got the old 1,1,2.

Probably nobody was as surprised as I was that the combo just sprung loose. Hell of a thing, muscle memory. Bang, bang. Bang. Two seconds, all right on the money. He even went down in a heap! The whole fight was like two seconds, literally. Last thing he expected to happen, that was a safe bet.

Hey, Sandy had me on a weight-lifting and weight-gaining regimen as well. She wouldn't let my skinny ass go to bed until I had finished this whole pot of mashed potatoes every night. It was a comprehensive makeover program. Ha! This straight outta prison scoundrel has just been completely polished off in less time than it takes to open a beer by a guy with a chest like a parakeet...

Didn't go over big with Kanzu.

He got a tire iron from his trunk and returned to the bar and I ran like hell. Police were called. Borzu told everyone he knew that he was going to kill me. Whatever. He was going to kill me for losing a fair fight that he provoked. C'mon man. Who does that? Not Borzu, I never saw him again. Somebody else did, though.

About 13 years later.

CHAPTER TWENTY-TWO:
AMAZING GRACE

"We are not human beings on a spiritual journey, we are spiritual beings on a human journey."
- Pierre Teilhard de Chardin

The first ten minutes.

The butcher knife slid in easily, right in the middle of my back meat. Like a big old turkey. When it was pulled I sensed a clean cut. I felt unfathomable, unprecedented amount of trouble as I could feel hot blood spurting into my ribcage from wounds on either side of the cut, underneath my skin. There was already tons of blood coming out and I was pretty sure I was going to die, doing the math of how long an ambulance would probably take to get there, the ride to the hospital, how much blood it felt like I was losing, etc. My stomach dropped as I heard and felt a gurgling noise in my back, like a wet sock squishing in rubber galoshes. "Somebody call an ambulance!" I bleated at the shocked onlookers. It was dusk on a crowded beachside street in Venice. There must have been about twenty people gathering around. It was kind of a tourist-y street that leads to the beach: sunglasses shops, bars, incense vendors. "Is anyone a doctor? Does anyone know first aid?" I was yelling, but I knew I had to cool out, and fast, if I was going to have any chance of surviving. [The first police on the scene later told me, in their experience, people with wounds similar to mine died 100% of the time]

My air was already limited so I figured my lungs were filling with blood. My breath was already short and very painful. I was going to have to conserve my energy and figure out how to extend my life until the ambulance arrived. I lowered myself to the ground and laid on my stomach. Pump, pump, pump went my blood. At this point, I found out later, both my lungs were punctured and an artery was cut. I was losing big-time amounts of blood. Mostly internal. I can't begin to describe how hard it was to breathe. "Somebody apply direct pressure to this wound!" I yelled. Somebody obliged.

Big mistake. It wasn't that kind of wound, as the damage was internal, and when the guy pressed his hand onto my back it just suffocated me more. It also made a sucking slurping sound. I realized that everything I thought my life was about was wrong. I was sure I was destined to persevere through tough times and make it big. I was sweating and my shirt was filling up with blood. I felt like crying. This was my death scene? Stabbed by a low-life on a dirty street in Venice, then I bleed to death?

The guy applying direct pressure was going to have to take a break. I was dying on a sidewalk in front of the Townhouse Tavern. "OK, stop that, that's not working." I rolled over onto my back where I just felt the blood squirting and squirting, almost like a faucet. I thought I felt my lungs sucking dirt off the pavement through the wound like a big mollusk, splurch, suck, splurt. I could feel every pump of my heart and a bunch was coming out every time. Every breath felt like the wind getting knocked out of me a little more.

I was taking little sips of air and trying to stay cool in the head, but JESUS CHRIST, the PAIN. Fuck, it really hurt. Like there were several badly broken bones in my back. My stomach hurt like I got kicked in the guts. The lungs and the bleeding were scaring the living shit out of me. I was sweating so much, a clammy death-sweat that felt gray in color. This was a very, very dirty, painful, prolonged torturous way to die. About three or four minutes had passed. I had been speared like a fish, skewered like a shish-kabob. The knife had gone in about 11 inches right through the center of my back, slipping off the spine and through both my lungs and nicking an artery.

A cop comes up, finally. "Do you know who did this to you?" "I don't care, get me a fucking ambulance, where is the fucking ambulance?!?!?" "They are on their way, who did this to you?" "Gasp-

148

GuynamedEnnis-gasp." My words were kind of coming out in little heaves now. "Ennis Miller? Black guy, rides a little electric motorcycle?" "Yeah." Just laying there on the sidewalk, chilling, waiting for an ambulance, dee-dee-dee. I cannot believe how much blood has come out and I'm still awake.

The ambulance arrives, four burly paramedics come up and start asking me questions. What's wrong, am I allergic to medicine, what kind of toothpaste I use. "Look, guys, GET ME TO THE FUCKING HOSPITAL!!!!!!!!" I was no Surgeon General here but I was pretty sure that I was going to bleed to death before I had any allergic reaction to Benedryl or Aspercreme or whatever.

I had a real good head start. I estimate by this time I had lost at least a liter of blood. A huge cut on your head that is bleeding like crazy might be an ounce or two at most… "Sure, buddy." I remember the strong capable hands putting me onto the gurney and loading it into the ambulance, the EMTs were doing their thing, giving me an IV of some sort. I can't remember what questions they were asking but I was getting angrier with every one. The stupid back wound kept squishing and pumping and I wanted to cry.

I was a strong man, 200 pounds of muscle and the weakness and sadness I felt I can never explain. The worst nightmare you can't detach from, each second an eternity. There is a panic and a slight hope but that hope is eclipsing with each passing second, that no matter how much I wanted to live, no matter how bravely I fought, that I was going to die, it was so obvious. The cop said the same later. She said, "We had seen so many fatalities in our line of work, that we know what people do and don't live through. We knew, as you left the scene, that you were dead."

The second ten minutes.

"Look, guys, I'm bleeding to death, you need to get me to a hospital ASAP, it's really that simple. It hurts to breathe, let me sit up a little, I don't

149

want to answer fucking questions because I just don't have the air, OK!?" That sentence was choked out in tortured half-breaths. "OK, buddy, let us do our job, you do your job." My job!? What exactly was my job now? Surviving. I kept moaning at them, WHERE IS THE FUCKING HOSPITAL? I knew there were closer hospitals. I suspected they were taking me somewhere far away because I was uninsured (not true). They asked me to stay laying down where my lungs and chest were becoming a lake of internal blood… every time the ambulance accelerated, turned or braked, it all went rushing into that direction, making my increasingly difficult breathing impossible. The pain and fear of dying were off the charts now. I kept yelling that I needed to sit up and interspersed that with my mantra, "Where The Fuck Are You Guys Taking Me? Where The Fuck Is the Hospital?!!!" And I told them that putting me onto my back was killing me (turns out later that I was right, but they have to do it that way). I was also back-seat driving and bitching and screaming whenever the guy lurched the ambulance, which was every ten seconds. I just envisioned this huge purple puddle swishing back and forth inside of me.

I was so much deader than alive, I have no idea why I was still alive, but I know why I hadn't lost consciousness: I **knew** that if I slipped away and stopped fighting that that was it. The only thing keeping me alive was the weird electricity or whatever that is your soul or your consciousness. Boy, these guys were sick of me and told me as much, they had probably never dealt with such an ungrateful know-it-all in their whole careers.

But I was dying, for real, gulping at air like a fish out of water and not enough was getting through my punctured lungs to keep me alive for any more than a few more seconds it seemed, but every few seconds passed and I was still there, and it got worse the whole time.

They wanted to just throw me out the back and drive away. They really did. A guy in front practically said so. It did not prevent them, however, from saving my life. "It's just around the corner, here it comes." He was bullshitting me because it was still another five minutes away… anything to get me to shut the fuck up.

The LAST FIVE minutes.

When we finally arrived I tried to patch it up with the EMTs: "Sorry guys, thank you, but you know I'm dying, that's why I'm being such a dick." "Sure, buddy, just live, OK?" I was still panicked but much more woozy now and still breathing. The EMTs were always checking my vitals and I think they were trying not to scare me when they would be like "Blood Pressure?" The other EMT would look at them like it was a subject you don't bring up at the dinner table, like "this guy doesn't really have any, let's not make a big federal case out of it right in front of him." I really wanted to cry so badly then but what was the point? I just stopped complaining and asked the EMT to hold my hand. This was it, I was going to die right there in that ambulance.

By this point I had lost about 3 LITERS of blood. Just the economy-size old two-liter bottle of blood, plus one more. But now I was surrounded by doctors and the tools and means of recovery. I was in great health (before I got stabbed), in a kick-ass hospital, and I was really confident that I would make it now… hey there's a bag of blood hangin there! I know I need that! They were sticking needles in, giving me transfusions, covering me with those little sticky monitors, all the stuff that was making me feel better when one of the doctors tells me there's going to be "some pain." "We have to insert a chest tube. It's going through your ribs." Have these guys ever heard of knocking a patient out? What was next, my leech bath?

He wasn't joking about the pain. Plus, the strangest thing happened next. There's this small Asian girl in a doctor coat on my left side looking all flustered like she just struck out at T-ball four at-bats in a row and the other doctors were coaching her, "Like, c'mon Anna!" GENERAL ANESTHETIC? Anyone? Wake me up when its over and there's flowers in my room and some hot oatmeal and oxycontin on tap? He was kind of explaining that general was dangerous but they were putting me out soon... the darkness finally came.

CHAPTER TWENTY-THREE:
COMMUNITY SERVICE
Laundromat Fight

THE second time I moved to Hollywood was in 2007, and I lived there with this very funny and odd recluse named Max who slept on the couch of his own 1- bedroom pad and charged me 700 for the bedroom. After making a fairly full recovery from the stab wound and building this crazy dude's Hollywood Hills mansion, I was back behind the financial eightball pretty much again, but having a good time. West Hollywood was simply a very fun place to live. I think because of the subject matter of this book, a reader might think I am kind of a miserable character: perennially broke and short-tempered. Maybe, but I have packed a lot of good times and laughs into this life, too. Enough for three or four people at least.

Our apartment, which was often scary dirty but next to a park, was in kind of a supernatural vortex of babes. West Hollywood is known for being a gay community, who are, as I have mentioned, the coolest neighbors in the world. It is also the center of the universe for acting and there are also a lot of models there. You would just see outrageously beautiful women at Ralph's, Trader Joes, Jiffy Lube and even friggin *Taco Bell,* for Christ's sake. I recall spotting Heidi Klum once at Whole Food's, and comparatively, she was maybe the second or even third hottest chick there at the time. [I can hear the Midwest dudes' bags packing right now... "I'm going to HOLLYWOOD!... er, I mean, WEST HOLLYWOOD!"] I guess I am some kind of weirdo, but being around a lot of beautiful women makes me feel happy and warm inside.

It is also a Russian community and our apartment was in a predominantly senior/Russian Jewish demographic. Max's grandma left him the apartment after she died. She was from Russia. I found Max where I have found everything else in life, on the awesome Craig's List!

153

[Max is a strange egg. He was very lonely, shy and a solitary dipsomaniac. However, after you got to know him, a lot of really cool things came out of that weird little guy. He was an inveterate punster, gourmet cook, king of mellow, an engineer of sorts, an expert on all things Punk Rock, and he counts among his friends members of the bands Berlin and The Silversun Pickups.]

There was a pretty fair amount of street crime in our neighborhood. I had like 9 bikes stolen and people would get stabbed or mugged periodically. We weren't in a BAD neighborhood, per se, but there were some sketchy pockets nearby [this applies to all of LA] and a lot of scum and trash filtered through our area.

I was doing laundry at the Laundromat on Sunset Blvd. one afternoon and all of a sudden this big commotion starts. A woman runs into the Laundromat and starts yelling, "STAY AWAY FROM ME, STAY AWAY FROM ME!" This hideously ugly black guy chases her into the place. I am on the computer they have there. He chases her inside and outta nowhere slugs her right in the jaw, POP! She kind of buckles and I get up, me and guy look at each other, frozen, and then he bolts out the door. I was a little frightened and confused about what to do. Clearly, I should have pounded the shit out the guy, but again, I froze [some tough guy, right?]

I sort of chase him a little ways down the street, just to see where he is going. There is a cop parked right outside and I offer to get in the unit with him to chase the guy down. The cop is not interested. He says something about waiting for something else, I don't know, maybe his dry cleaning or maybe he's staking out a double cheeseburger. I finally get his ass in gear, but it's too late. The perp is gone.

Incidentally, cops in major cities do not get that pumped about fistfights or simple assaults. If they did, I would have gotten the electric chair by now.

I return to the laundromat a little, no a lot ashamed. The woman thanks me, but I let a golden opportunity to display some of the skills I have been detailing for your reading pleasure slip away. The woman gave me the back story after she filed her police report:

The guy was harassing her and making suggestive comments so she told him to "get lost", which he didn't take well. He started following her around so she ran into the Laundromat for refuge, where he took the opportunity, as a gallant gentleman, to prove that he was a proper and respectful candidate for her attentions by socking her in the jaw.

He was very dark-skinned, about 6'2, maybe 175 pounds. He had crazy reddish eyes, oily little pigtails, weird chipmunk cheeks and scars on his face.

I just kind of felt like a coward and stewed about it for a few days. Shortly thereafter, I saw the guy standing outside a 7-11 in our neighborhood and called the cops. The police were completely disinterested in reopening The Case of the Chick Who Got Punched Two Weeks Ago.

I DESPERATELY WANTED NO MORE TROUBLE IN MY LIFE... BUT I FEEL LIKE I DON'T ALWAYS GET TO MAKE EVERY DECISION. But what fiendish God would compel me to start trouble with YET ANOTHER dangerous loser? My God, your God, our God?

D: All of the above.

I don't know how many more times I saw the dude, who was probably dealing drugs outside the 7-11. A couple more at least, and each time I just wanted to punch his ugly lights out.

One night I'm at the bar next to the 7-11 called Happy Endings. I am pretty buzzed. I walk over to 7-11 to get some gum. The guy is standing there. I don't think he recognized me. In fact, I'm sure he didn't, but I really didn't look that hard at him. I suppose I didn't want to spoil the surprise gift I had for him.

I walked to where I am just even with him and I whirl and unload a vicious right hook square on the guy's jaw.

It was a pretty good punch. The location was good, too. Right where the jaw hinge meets the neck or whatever. He crumpled onto his ass and held his jaw like he didn't know what the hell.

"**That** was for punching that chick at the Laundromat." Looking back, it would have been much cooler to just let him wonder. Let him think that every time he saw any big blonde surfer-looking guy it was time to duck. It would have fried the circuits of his tiny brain. Yeah, handsome white guys just go around slugging the hell out of gangsters in Los Angeles all the time for no reason. I hope I broke his jaw. It's possible. When I hit him it made a very weird noise.

He actually made it to his feet and took a couple swipes at me and when I went after him again he beat a hasty retreat. The guard at the 7-11 told me to get out of there before he called the cops. [How ungrateful. That guard should have invited me in and treated me to some Hostess Donettes and a cold High Gravity Malt Liquor for chasing off the perennial scum that adorned his storefront.] Fuck, they let Wyatt Earp friggin run the casino after performing the same kind of service in Tombstone. I didn't even rate a Slurpee?!?!

For a few months, I was worried that the thug was going to come back and shoot me or stab me or something. I was very leery around that area.

The guy was never seen again in front of that 7-11 (the security guards told me this). If I didn't break his jaw, I guarantee he had trouble chewing for a while. He obviously had a tough time chewing on the idea that he could get popped in the jaw any old

time he stood in front a 7-11, Circle K or AM/PM Mini
Market.

Dad —

CHAPTER TWENTY-FOUR:
MATCHING WITS WITH A GYPSY

OK, I have been skirting a fairly painful subject in this autofightography, or whatever it is. The subject is my father's death in 1986 when I was working at the car wash. It was horrible and I will spare you the gory details, but make sure you do not die of alcoholism if you can help it. My dad was a handsome guy who looked a bit like Alan Alda. He had a lot of demons and too much regret, shame and conscience for whatever sins he believed he had ever committed, which amounted to obeying the law, paying his taxes and providing for his family. Quite a rap sheet. He was a successful executive who I believe did not enjoy his job and became lonely and despondent. This malady probably kills millions of American men every year.

My dad, in his infinite wisdom, left all three of us kids about $100,000 each. What was smart was that he left it to us in three separate increments so we wouldn't blow it all at once. Me and my younger sister just blew the smaller amounts three times over [Paaaaar-Tee!!]. My older sister, like the pig who builds his house out of brick, didn't blow hers. She got married and had kids and I'm sure it paid for all kinds of mortgage bills, trips to Ross and whatnot.

Some of that money fueled my scuba instructor's schooling [money-blowing phase 2.0] and move to Hawaii, so it wasn't a total waste. I bought a very cool car with a portion of my first increment of my inheritance. I have always been ashamed of blowing the money (way to build on pop's legacy!), so I have skirted the topic. After all, this book is called "FIGHTEY-TOWN," not "DUMBASS-VILLE," but that might as well be the sequel.

My new ride was a 1969 red cougar convertible. I think I paid about 4 grand for it and it was a total lemon. I put a bunch of money into the front end and you better be ready to do the same if you buy a similar Mercury or Ford [Fix Or Repair Daily, hyuk,

hyuk] of that era. But that car was drop-dead sexy and fast. To this day, it was the most I ever spent on a car. My dad could only die so many times.

I was running out of inheritance 1.0, but working in a bar as a bartender at the time, so I wasn't panicking. But I wanted to sell the car. It was a reminder of my foolishness and it was a financial sinkhole more needy than a dependent child. I also could walk to work. I had dented it so I think I had a FOR SALE sign on it for about 2 grand. I get a call one day and a guy tells me that he is interested. He tells me to meet him at his apartment building, which was a four-plex right around the corner from where I was living at the time on Chicago's Near North Side.

I meet the guy, who is hilarious and charming. He comes out of the entryway of the four-plex as I ring the doorbell and he takes me out to lunch. The guy's name was DJ Metlow. He was a kind of good-looking and dark guy who was about 5'9" and 175 pounds, maybe 40 years old.

He took me to a local deli and bought me lunch and told me a bunch of hilarious stories. I forget what we talked about, but I remember that I was glad to be unloading this car to this dude who looked like he was going to become a friend of mine, too.

He got me down on the asking price and said he wanted to give it to his son for his birthday, which was tomorrow. Problem was, he only had 300 bucks deposit, but could he take the car and give me like the other 1200 next week?

Sure! I thought, we were already friends and all. Only problem was that I had lost the title. He even came over to my apartment to help me look for it, but we never found it. No problem, he said, we could just go down to the DMV, apply for a new title, which we could send to his address. He seemed to have an intricate knowledge of these dealings. I remember when I couldn't get a DMV employee on the phone from my apartment, he was like "Try the next number in the

160

sequence, if the last 4 digits are 3007, try like 3008, 3009, etc."

So that was how I unloaded the car. The title was going to his address but I could trust him. I had his phone number and I knew where he lived. Plus, we **were friends and all.** Are you sensing anything could be wrong, young Sherlock Holmes?

A few days later, I am out on a date. I am walking near his house and I went up and rang the bell to see if he was home. I was going to hit him up for like 50 bucks just to tide me over. I think I wanted him to meet the girl, too. She was pretty hot.

I rang the doorbell and some dude comes out. I asked him which unit DJ lived in. He told me that no DJ lived in that building. I asked him if he was certain. The little dominos that fell in my brain ruined the date, to say the least.

DJ never lived there, he just came out of the entryway. There was no son, there was no car, there was no more money coming, the title was going to some address I didn't know and I was also starting to seriously contemplate the possibility that Santa Claus had actually been my parents all along. This guy had played me like a Stradivarius.

NOT SO FAST! I had his phone number. In addition, some girl I had gone out with used to date a cop and SHE had given me this number that you could call, read the phone number to the operator and they would give you the address. I called my secret number and the address I got was a video store and what I did next was totally crazy.

I had dressed up as a black person for the last Halloween, even fooling some of my best friends with the make-up. I got some more of the makeup and put on a scroungy old suit and pretended to be a homeless black man in order to stake out the video store. I sat outside the store, like a bum, waiting for DJ to show up there! Talk about a kid who grew up watching too much TV… maybe I had seen Gene Wilder and Richard Pryor in "Silver Streak" one too many times.

DJ never showed up, and neither did anyone who looked like they might be his family member. The store was owned by Indians or Pakistanis.

This obviously was not this con-man's first scam. His phone number was cross-indexed to an address that wasn't his. That's why he gave it so freely.

A better plan hit me. Get to work and stop fucking around in life? Hell no!

I would call DJ and tell him that *I found the title* and he could come over and get it. He would have no idea that I discovered his scam and he would still think I was a clueless mark who was going to make his life easier by giving him the title so he could cash the car in for a healthy profit. What a maroon, he must have thought, as I excitedly told him that I found the title and he could come right over and get it. He bit.

So I told old DJ to come over and give me the rest of the dough, if for some reason he actually had it. If he showed up with my money, I would have felt foolish and been pleasantly surprised. If he showed up and asked for the title without having any more money, I would know that I had been scammed.

If that was the case, I had plans for DJ that did not include a stern lecture from me about the true meaning of friendship that would make him break down in tears and promise to give up his life of crime so we could open up a pretzel stand together. I wasn't *that* stupid.

I was PISSED. I am a pretty intelligent and cynical guy, and even as a kid, I did not get hustled that often. I was VERY bummed about losing the 1200 bucks, but what really got me boiling was the way he hustled me.

He used my friendly spirit against me. All of our great conversation and chumminess was just his technique to beat me out of my car. I wasn't prepared for this emotionally. We didn't have gypsies in Glen Ellyn and they never covered this type of situation on The Brady Bunch. I'm not sure why, but that was what made me so angry that I had no hesitation to do what I did next.

DJ called me to tell me that he was on his way. I asked him if he was going to have my cash. He said there was a little problem with that but he could get it for me soon, but his son couldn't even drive the car on his birthday because it wasn't registered blah blah blah. I told him no problem, come and get the title, I *trusted* him, he was my pal, come on over, I was just happy to get it to him, maybe we can hang out, bake cupcakes, watch some Rockford Files reruns.

Boy, was I excited when I hung up the phone. I was running *a successful con on a fucking gypsy.*

DJ must have had some warning bells go off somewhere because he looked extremely nervous when he rang my doorbell and said he was sorry that he couldn't stay long, that he was in a hurry. Sure, no problem, I said, smiling like the Mr. Roarke from Fantasy Island. I invited him in with a grand sweep of my hand.

He walked in the door nervously and took a right in front of me to walk down a short hallway.

I grabbed him by the back of his navy blue hoodie and slammed him headfirst into a wall and then back the other way so his head hit the other wall then back over to the first wall. BANG!! BONK! BOINGIING! His head hit each wall very hard.

I spun him around and hit him with a very hard right straight into his face. He began screaming and scrambling on my floor like a wounded animal. This is the difference between real fights and movie fights, where one cowboy hits another one and knocks the guy unconscious. His head had been slammed hard three times and he had absorbed a point blank right from a kid who could punch. It didn't knock him out, like Gilligan getting hit with a coconut by The Skipper, it made him scream and fight for his life like a raccoon with rabies. As he was screaming at me "OH PATRICK WHY ARE YOU DOING THIS!" I was screaming, "IT WAS ALL A FUCKING SCAM," while he replied, while really getting his ass kicked, "NO SCAM PATRICK NO SCAMMMM."

It wasn't going at all how I had planned. I thought I would pound him and he would start crying or whatever and give me back my car. He just kept scrambling around on my floor as I punched him. I spied a thick cane that I had used when I had hurt my foot. It was pretty heavy-duty, like an inch thick, and solid. I picked it up and hit him as hard as I could on top of his head with it, figuring it would knock him out. It just made this horrible wooo-COORRKKK sound of a base hit as I cracked him square on top of his skull as he was on all fours. It didn't remotely sound like I hit a person with it, it sounded like I hit a picket fence as hard as I could with that cane.

Did the guy go out? NO! His wailing just went up about four octaves and it made him redouble his scrambling efforts. If you have ever seen video of people trying to catch a greased pig at the county fair, that's what it looked like. Blood was getting all over the place from where the cane hit him in the head. This was turning into a nightmare.

So I drag him, screaming and wailing, by his shirt out of my apartment and he his shrieking about calling the cops. I throw him into the phone booth in the lobby and said, "Go ahead, asshole." And just kind of squinched the door shut until the cops got there, which seemed like about four seconds later. There is blood everywhere, all over me, the carpet and on the windows of the phone booth. The cops come up to the building and I drag him outside.

A female cop gets out of the unit and holds a chrome-plated .38 at my face from about six feet

164

away. I let go of him and he is screaming about how I tried to kill him. OK, I am about to get shot to death now.

The female cop goes, "So where is he shot?" The fuckin guy told them that I had shot him. The other cop gets out his wallet, and I swear like fifty IDS unroll out of the plastic...he looks at his partner and says, "THIS GUY's A FUCKIN GYPSY!!"

CHAPTER TWENTY-FIVE:
A COUPLE OF HIGH SCHOOL FIGHTS

I WENT TO GLENBARD WEST HIGH SCHOOL, A school that is so idyllic and beautiful, that it is actually the location of a 1986 [two years after I graduated] Hollywood movie called "Lucas," starring the insufferable [according to a friend who worked on the movie] Corey Haim. He was, however, excellent in his role as the title character. "Lucas" is the story of a quirky, undersized misfit that tries out for the football team to impress a girl. It is a sweet and completely watchable movie. Here is a truly bizarre anecdote:

When the producers happened upon the location [God knows how, Glen Ellyn being 2000 miles from Hollywood], they hired quite a few of the locals to fill out the cast. Cheerleaders, coaches and regular students got to be extras in the film, which also featured pre-fame Charlie Sheen and Winona Ryder.

There was one student who made the most of his acting opportunity. His name was Tom Hodges. Tom parlayed his role in Lucas to a decent C-list actor's career. Tom had quite a few speaking lines as Lucas' chief bully. He was very convincing as Lucas' large and vocal tormentor. I thought the casting was excellent, because Tom Hodges had gone to my grade school, Hawthorne Elementary. Tom had been, in almost the exact same way as in the movie, **my actual bully in grade school.** I didn't like being bullied and I took my older sister's green Girl Scout pocket knife to school one day to stab Tom Hodges, or maybe it was to kill my other bully, Rob Crockett. Thankfully, I never did the shanking or I might STILL be in some mental institution, only to escape on Halloween to slice up buxom teenage girls in evermore depressing sequels and remakes.

I think the kids at Glenbard West were kind of above fighting for the most part. We had an absolutely amazing high school class that actually *occasionally* blurred the strict "popularity" clique lines and all got drunk together at house parties. There wasn't too much squabbling, as everyone was really trying to just find someone that would make out with them. The maturity level of the 14 to 17 year-olds I hung out with was much higher than the general standard of decorum I would find among grown-assed adults at Hollywood night clubs a couple decades later.

I was the class clown, and I was actually given my own section of the school paper where I made fun of everything at the school. I was once even called onto the carpet by a Drivers Ed teacher I had made fun of in the high comic style you have been enjoying so much. After reading the article that Chip Dempsey and I wrote about his Insult Comic teaching style, Don Burns told us that he wanted to "get his shotgun." In my finest moment, I told the sarcastic bastard that he had no trouble dishing it out, so he shouldn't have any taking it. I was officially elected "Funniest Guy In School" for senior honors. Nobody thought of me as a tough guy, probably, but I could carve your ass up with some mean roasting skilz, the pen being truly mightier than the suh-woard, Gentle Reader!

But there **were** a couple of fights, now that I think about it.

I got this great after-school job at Reuss Sporting Goods in "Downtown" Glen Ellyn. It was an overpriced suburban dealer of All Things Sports, owned by "Old Man Reuss" who was from Texas and was the only person in Illinois that wore a cowboy hat, which I thought was bad-ass. Reuss was sports apparel-oriented, riding the wave of the Sweat Pants Revolution of the mid-eighties [Yes, you can thank me now, senior citizens]. Employees at Reuss wore jeans and a shirt and tie, which I thought was a rad way to dress. It was a ridiculously easy job that mainly consisted of making a half-assed effort at hawking basketballs and Converse high-tops [the most uncomfortable shoe ever manufactured] while making sure I kept one of the awesomely cool managers laughing all day. I did that to keep them from making good on their promise to fire me if I didn't start caring. The gig was kind of ruined for me when they hired the girl I had a crush on since I was four years old, the sublimely gorgeous and hilarious Heather Wayt. *It killed* me to be around her, Tantalus had nothing on 16-year-old PD. I had to see her every day and know she was going out with and probably getting banged by her handsome and popular boyfriend.

My violent streak was fairly dormant during this phase of my life, but I still held the secret belief that the middleweight boxing champion's belt was being held by some pretender like Sugar Ray Leonard or Marvin Hagler, who were just keeping it warm for me. I shadow-boxed all throughout my youth, getting ready to knock one of their asses out in the first round as soon as they stopped ducking me. At sixteen, I was probably about 5'11" and 140 pounds, built like a ski jumper or an anorexic heroin model.

One Saturday afternoon, this jerky kid name Kenny is making faces at me through the shop windows and flipping me off. A circuit jumped inside me. I didn't know the kid even vaguely. I went outside to ask him what the hell his problem was. He said he thought I was a dick or something. I asked him if he wanted to hash it out man-to-man. He told me that was precisely what he had in mind.

I was wearing tan Adidas rugby pants, a maroon oxford, my cranberry knit tie with the square bottom, and penny loafers [I wonder how much you would have to pay me to wear that around for a week now? *A lot* is the answer.] I don't know why the hell I remember this stuff, but I always do. It was a bright and sunny day, and nobody was shuddering in any kind of howling arctic wind or shuffling around three feet of slush in a frozen fog of pain, so it must have been near summertime.

I walked out, squared up and threw the combination I had been practicing in my bedroom that was intended for Roberto Duran's chin. It worked, unbelievably. People have asked me why I have won so many fights. Part of it is because I often fight people that are very drunk, but it also might have something to do with speed and accuracy. All the punches landed in his face with a satisfying thud. The blows couldn't have had *too much power* as I was bench-pressing in the high 90-pound range at that time.

I think it was two jabs and a straight right and it had old Kenny pinwheeling around and grabbing for a clinch that ripped my shirt pocket. He split the scene wisely under his own power with a black eye and the best part was that old Heather witnessed the whole thing! It only took about 40 seconds from start to finish, with considerable style points for returning to work unscathed save for the pocket that Heather got a safety pin and fixed for me! My boss, who was downstairs during the brawl, never even found out! I probably masturbated about Heather an *extra* seven times that night. [I hope someone has the good sense to edit that last part out, for poor Heather's sake].

My second and last fight of my high school career was with rival funnyman, Quinton Porter. Quinton was a big fat kid who did a great Jake Blues routine in a school assembly once. We weren't really friends or enemies. We were both very funny kids who never gave each other credit. Professional courtesy. Somehow we ended up sitting at the same table at McDonald's one night [Jesus, the God damn restaurant figures in a lot of my fights... hormone-packed anger-inducing bill of faire?] We were trying to out-joke each other around a table of mutual friends and began an impromptu roast of each other. The duel got ugly. Quinton said something about me that completely pissed me off. Then I went WAY out of line with him. I eyed his chest lustily and said:

"Quinton, your man-tits are making me so horny that it's driving me crazy, would you please get a bra or something?" The joke killed, so I piled it on: "Can I get some Aunt Jemima for those flapjacks?" Wow, I told you I could be a mean kid.

Quinton turned red and just got up and left the table. I thought that I had vanquished my foe! But Quinton walked behind me and did something really unsportsmanlike: He chewed up some French fries, spit them into his hand and slapped them on the back of my neck.

GROSSSSSSSSSSSSSSSSSS!!!!!!!!!!!!!!!!!!!!!!

He kind of fled outside. I went out to the parking lot, furious, unleashing a hellish fusillade of swear words and epithets all ending or containing the phrase "fat fuck." Quinton and I kind of squared up and I unloaded the old 1,2,3 dead into his face. Quinton then went berserk and several people went to restrain him to prevent him from killing me. He had to outweigh me by at least 100 pounds. I think my friend hurried me to a car and got me out of there while about fifty people were holding Quinton back.

Quinton sported a black eye for a while and he and I returned to an uneasy truce. I was always worried that he would smash me to pieces one day. A year later, when I received the "Funniest Guy" award, Quinton approached me for the first time since our fight... to congratulate me!

Class move, old boy, class move!

Again, my high school days were singularly non-violent. I think I spent the entire 4-year period in a very uncomfortable red haze of unsatisfied sexual lust that kept key portions of my psyche pre-occupied at all times.

171

CHAPTER TWENTY-SIX:
ANOTHER TIME THAT I GOT JUMPED

YOU KNOW, if I were king and in charge of the criminal justice system, as a king would be, there would be a few changes: Guys and gals jailed or imprisoned for any kind of non-violent crime [drugs, theft, probation violation... 80% of the prison population] would have their sentences drastically reduced, while violent offenders might end up with more time.

As King Of the United States, I would also have secret cars on the freeway, and high-speed tailgaters would get pulled over, have a judge watch a video via satellite of their shenanigans and, if convicted, a mobile unit would be dispatched to the scene and would crush their car into a cube. A reminder sign would be planted in the cube at the site of the offense. If the idiot was caught driving in the breakdown lane at 90 miles an hour flashing his brights at everyone to move of their way a *second time*, they would simply be burned at the stake like a witch, right at the side of the freeway. I have this little theory that these people cause about 95% of the fatalities on the road.

I have a similar sympathy for people who "jump" people. By that, I mean, those who jump in on a fight like a cowardly hyena, to get their blows in while the guy they are attacking is otherwise occupied trying to fight another person; it's only happed to me about 6 times. Those hooligans in Kalamazoo were the first ones. It happened to me again in Hawaii, Hollywood, Venice, Hollywood and Hollywood again. I'm not going to get into the details of the Venice Incident because it contains some possibly unfinished business...

The other tales of uber-macho strangers conspiring to beat me half to death I am more than happy, nay ecstatic, to relate to you.

Getting jumped in Hollywood.

This was right around the time I fought Doctor Mansonbum. You could say I was leading the life of a true sheltered aristocrat. My life was about as productive and prestigious as a towel boy's in a Mexican whore house.

One night, I took the long walk from The Cockroach Arms to this bar called Red Rocks on Sunset Boulevard. I went by myself to try to meet a girl. As well as I had been doing a few months prior in Laguna was as badly as I was striking out in Hollywood. I mean, it could have been the flashing neon "LOSER" sign the girls were picking up on. They couldn't *know* I was brewing my coffee in the sink of a Hobo Hilton with hot water through a dirty washcloth and surviving on the under-sweetened Mexican wallboard cakes I could buy 3 for 29 cents… but it seeped through maybe that I hadn't just stepped out of my helicopter a few minutes earlier.

I shined myself up as well as I could, maybe threw on my one decent shirt and pair of jeans, fortified my courage with a couple delicious 40s of Bud Ice and went on a ladyhunt! And for once during that Winter of My Discontent I was succeeding. I was talking to a pretty young thang when I was rudely interrupted by a small, young gent of Middle Eastern parentage, who told me:

"HEY, BODDY, YEAH I'M TALKING TO YOU BODDY. THAT GIRL, SHE DOESN'T WANT TO TALK TO YOU ANYMORE. DON'T IGNORE ME BODDY, I AM TALKING TO YOU."

"I'm sorry, is she your girlfriend?" The girl shakes her head "no," but I had the vague feeling that she knew him. I replied:

"Well, dude, she doesn't have any problem with me talking to her, and since we are in America, she can do whatever she wants."

"I'M TELLING YOU BODDY, GET THE FUCK OUT OF HERE IF YOU KNOW WHAT IS GOOD FOR YOU."

174

I informed him that he watched too much television and real people didn't talk that way. We had a little back and forth that ended up with me asking him to step outside, and he said:

"FOCK YEAH, BODDY, I WILL BE KICKING YOUR ASS SO FUCKING HARD IN JUST A MINUTE, YOU WILL REGRET THE DAY YOU WERE BORN."

But he didn't follow me out the door. I came back and asked him what the fuck was going on. It was time to put up or shut up. Clearly.

"LOOK ASSHOLE, DON'T WORRY THERE WILL BE YOUR ASS GETTING KICKED OUTSIDE THIS CLUB. I WILL PUNCH YOU IN YOUR FUCKING FACE TO A PULP, BODDY, YOUR MOTHER WILL NOT RECOGNIZE YOU."

I tried to shame him into stepping outside but I just got another blast of:

"DON'T WORRY, YOUR FUCKING ASS IS GRASS BITCH AND-

I had heard quite enough, Gentle Reader and I interrupted his fairly convincing soliloquy with a very satisfying right hand that caught him square in the nose with a resounding "SQUISH-POP", which was hopefully the sound of his nose breaking. I was unaware that his buddies had now surrounded me and they all began teeing off on me at the same time.

This was one of my best fights.

I knew that getting tossed to the ground was the last thing that I wanted to happen so I just kind of stayed on my feet and slugged it out with the four of them. The fight spilled out on Sunset Boulevard, where the cowardly swarm and I fought pretty much to a draw until a bystander reached over the railing and choked one of them while the crowd stopped the other two or three. I stood there panting and screamed at them in triumph;

YOU FUCKIN **PUSSIES,** FOUR OF YOU COULDN'T EVEN TAKE ME OUT, FOUR OF YOU!!!!

Oh yes, I was riding high as I walked the 20 blocks down to my roach filled abode. Fire up the trumpets! Pour the finest wine, slaughter the pigs! Winner and grand champion of the Idiot Olympics returneth to Nowhereville to nobody in triumph. A few days later I was relaying the story to a guy I knew from high school. He was living in Hollywood and actually succeeding in life and wanted nothing to do with me on a social basis.

As I showed him the scrape marks on my ribs and recounted my tale of bravery, he had a curious look on his face. I was expecting him to laugh and laud the derring-do of this broken down 35-year-old pugilist. He just looked shocked and saddened.

Saddened!? Didn't he think it was *cool* that I went toe-to-toe with four dudes for no reason whilst residing in a bum hotel while **he** was out wasting his time building a productive life? Some people just have their priorities out of whack.

CHAPTER TWENTY-SEVEN:
FIGHT AT LAKE ELLYN

IT MUST HAVE BEEN 6th grade, and my best friend at the time was Chris Till. Chris was absolutely hilarious and he had this super strong Amazon older sister named Hilary who I think I had a crush on. How do I know that Hilary was super-strong? Once we were all play-fighting and she actually picked me up and threw me at Chris, knocking him to the ground. She picked me up sideways and threw me at Chris, like you would throw a large log onto a bonfire, and that probably gave me a boner for a week, OK, three months.

Chris and I were walking across a field at Lake Ellyn Park, an incredibly beautiful park with a man-made lake, a boathouse and dock, and oak trees that were around 400 feet tall. We were just passing through when we happened upon some other area youth. For some reason, both parties began an angry dialog, possibly of the "what are you looking at" variety. The kids were from the HATED rival elementary school, Ben Franklin, and we may have had some issues with them being on our "turf." My school, Hawtorne, had beaten BF in football because we ruled at football, but a 52-to-8 beatdown by their hoops squad prompted me to petulantly and blatantly trip their star guard, Dave Woody, onto his face at the end of the game. Some of the parents laughed like the post-apocalypse savages did in "The Road Warrior" when the guy gets his fingers chopped off by the feral child's boomerang.

YET I DIGRESS! I think there were three of them and two of us, and being men of honor, it was decided that I would square off with Jeff Berenschot. There was some circling and punching but in the end I got him in a headlock.

177

The fight ended quickly with me choking Jeff silly. I was a cunning and savage child with a bizarre and vicious fighting instinct. Three years later, Jeff and I would compete every week to see who would represent the 112 pound Glenbard West's freshman wrestling team. Jeff beat me every single time because he was stronger than I was, but I had the edge that day in the park due to my aggression, amorality and willingness to murder another child on General Principles.

Jeff gave up, and the fight was halted. Chris and I walked away in triumph when Jeff punched me as hard as he could in the head from behind. I just shook it off and kept walking. Victory was mine. He lost. I won. His huffy, illegal, and cowardly post-fight cuff was just another black mark on **his** record, not mine.

Being young men of class and distinction, Jeff and I never brought the incident up again when we attended the same Junior High School together the next year. We even sat at the same lunch table and became friends. Jeff was a good-natured and cool kid despite the unmanly late blow.

Nobody would have believed me anyway. Jeff was known as a very tough kid in his neighborhood. I was known as a mouthy little punk, which is exactly what I was.

LATER THAT YEAR

With my nuts fully swollen from the Jeff Berenschot victory, I began telling a girl that I liked, Sharon Griffin, what a stud I was during class. [Chris Till actually went out with her in sixth grade and threw up on her while riding the Tilt-A-Whirl at the carnival, much to my delight]. There was a guy named Mark Donaldson that was a year or two older than I was, and Sharon was telling me how cute she thought he was. I told her that I could kick his ass pretty easily. I'm not sure how I made that transition in the conversation, but whatever, I guess I felt it needed to be said. Never mind that Mark Donaldson had only ever been cool to me and everyone else. Sharon liked him so she needed to know, if the chips were down, that his ass was grass and I was a lawnmower.

A few days later, I was walking home from school and Mark Donaldson, looking the Picture of Cool, as usual, in his faded jeans, flannel shirt and Addidases, cuts across the parkway to halt my progress down the sidewalk, using his forest green Schwinn Varsity as a barricade. [I bought an ancient Schwinn Varsity at a garage sale a couple years back, the thing still drove like a Lamborghini.] He broke it down for me right there in front Mark LeRoy's house. Mark Donaldson had curly blonde hair like The Greatest American Hero.

"Hey, Davis, Sharon Griffin tells me you can kick my ass." Sharon, you little BITCH! My usually fast-thinking brain was just flashing BUSTED...BUSTED...BUSTED.

"Nah, you, well, hey, ah....the the, uh"

"Well, if you are going to kick my ass, here's your chance, I'm right here."

Where was this confrontational tough-guy side coming from? Mark was Mr. Mellow. His jaw was clenching and he looked pretty worked up.

"No, I ah"

"Sharon Griffin said that you told her that you could kick my ass, now I'm right here. So why don't you kick my ass, Davis? Hey, Davis, you listening to me?"

"See...um...the...I was just talking uh, I don't think I even s-" My legs were shaking pretty badly.

"You were talking **shit,** huh? Well don't talk shit anymore, got it, Davis? You got it, Davis?" He

179

looked at me with contempt for about twenty more terrifying seconds, letting his words sink in and then he rode away. Cuz that's how Mark Donaldson handled his business.

What an invaluable lesson learned! No, not the lesson that Sharon Griffin was a loose-lipped bitch, although that was all I could think about on my walk home and for the next few days. The lesson that stuck was:

FIGHTING TIP NUMBER FOURTEEN: Talking a bunch of shit that you can't back up is pointless, dangerous and *makes* *you* look like a bitch.

CHAPTER TWENTY-EIGHT:
I LEARNED NOTHING IN RECOVERY

EMAIL BETWEEN MY SIS AND I
IN THE WEEKS AFTER I WAS STABBED:

Hum,

Thought I was going to bounce out of this like it was a scrape you get riding your bike, not quite. I set the new hospital record for vicodin consumption as I tried to resume a normal life, turns out I was masking pain (sometimes pain is your friend). Taking two, three at a time and riding my bike. Got to spend the next few days cut off pain meds and pretty much realllllllly bumming out on the couch. Then I get the worst news ever, some intern I call on the phone tells me there's like a ten percent chance that I live the rest of my life in this agonizing pain...think I'm getting better now. They severed some major nerves and stuff when they peeled me like a shrimp getting into my chest cavity. FUCK! This will not do me any good in the rage-a-holic phase when I get healthy...mebbe it wll...anger is wasted energy anger is wasted energy.

Welp, got out of the old house now and walked to the local coffee shop, shoulda stayed in bed. Drop me a line and find out when I regain my 4.4 speed and Tom Sawyer-type good luck!
Stay tuned!

Anne Lange <XXXX@yahoo.com> wrote:

Thank God you are still alive after that. I hope that guy gets ass raped every day in prison.
I love you,
Anne

RECOVERY

Semi-permanent nerve damage, shooting pains that lasted almost a year, intermittent bouts of rage at what had happened. A permanent dead spot on top of my ribcage. If I was a car with that level of damage, it would have been scrapped.

In the aftermath, I also had time to contemplate how horrible it would be for my mother to have to bury her son. I saw my grandma have to bury my father, and it was truly horrifying. And to be killed by such a worthless piece of human garbage like Ennis, who that genius Claire married, by the way, while he was in prison. He got six years. I don't think that was enough time. Not for what he did. I mean, we have to keep room in our jails for the guys who sell bags of coke to Hollywood bimbos because they get 60 years.

My friends and family would have had the burden of my death to carry around: The pointless death of a brilliant loser.

I ran into one of Ennis's friends at a party a year after the stabbing. He told me that Ennis had told everyone that I had slapped his girlfriend and that he was just defending her. By stabbing me in the back. Me, a famous brawler who had stood up for women and the homeless, had punched a girl, while Ennis the Famous Coward, had not defended her at the time but had chosen to stab me in the back as I rode away. The guy started off the conversation angry with me. He ended up hugging me and telling me that Ennis' story hadn't really made any sense to anyone.

I ran into one of the ambulance drivers on the boardwalk. I hugged him. It was very emotional.

In the weeks after I survived, I was almost in an enchanted land sometimes. Children's laughter sounded very musical. The sunshine on my face felt like a drug. Every breath seemed like a gift from God. Indeed it was. Indeed it is.

Two Venice cops stopped me on my bike one night about four months after it all went down. I thought I was going to receive a ticket for riding my bike without a light. The cop told me that I was famous around the station house for what I had said in Ennis's pretrial. He asked me if what he had heard that I said was true, it was.

Ennis eventually took a plea deal, but his attorney was badgering me during the hearing and I got impatient. He had asked me if I had planned to use my bike as a weapon and all this other ridiculous shit. He asked me what happened after I struck Ennis in our fight. I remembered a line from a hard-boiled detective novel, it went something like:

"Ennis went down faster than a ten-Peso hooker." It was fun to say in court. However, I owe an apology to Ten-Peso hookers everywhere. Unlike Ennis, at least they have a fuckin' job.

CHAPTER TWENTY-NINE:
THE COMEBACK

"Pushing up the ante, I know you wanna see me,
Read 'em and weep, the dead man's hand again,
I see it in your eyes, take one look and die,
The only thing you see, you know it's gonna be,
The Ace Of Spades." - Motorhead

"Don't judge a book by its cover!!" - anon

The 14-inch butcher punctured both my lungs but the only long-term damage was to a major nerve in my back. I believed because of my injuries that I would never be the same fighter again. I could still play sports and everything, but it took the work of an amazing healer [Yvonne Kriens] to get me over the chronic nerve pain and after the two draws, after like a 30 fight win streak, I assumed my street-fightin' days were behind me. Part of me was saddened, part of me relieved. I just guessed that this special snap and speed that gave me that critical split-second advantage was gone, and it was best to knock it off before I really got hurt or killed.

I acknowledged that it was time to hang up the badge, Walker. Maybe concentrate on something slightly more productive, like making some damn money like a normal adult.

One warm night in 2008, I was riding my bicycle, my only wheels at the time, up on Sunset Boulevard after the bars closed at 2 a.m. Cruising for babes per usual, on a bike! [not the motorized kind] on the Sunset Strip!! 'Cause that's the kind of ride the short-skirt wearing hotties are looking for, right? I was wearing these ridiculous green pants and a bright yellow terry cloth shirt. I may have no longer been a fighter, but I still dressed like I didn't give a fuck what you thought. I wasn't giving up that privilege.

Anyway, this group of guys is also milling around: Three small white guys and one gigantic black kid. One of the white kids tells me it's a cool bike. That was nice. I mean, it's not the beach, so you don't usually see a bright red brand new beach cruiser rolling around. I stopped to talk to these girls that were parked in a BMW, when the group of guys approached. They are kind of trying to hone in on my good vibe with the ladies, not cool, the quadruple cock-block, but I don't really care.

Then the giant black kid [6'4", 250] says to the girls, "Why you talking to this guy? All he got is this raggedy bike, I got a Lexus." WHAT?! Nice job, douche. Not only have you insulted, for no reason, the guy who got the ball rolling for your dumb ass, but you also have scared the gazelles from the watering hole. He has spoiled the mood for everyone.

The girls kind of laugh awkwardly and say goodbye.

I am pissed, but the kid is way too big to fuck with and, besides, I have retired. But I do say to him,

"You know, that wasn't too respectful, what you said."

The words were chosen carefully. Many violent and tough guys when looking to avoid trouble bring it down to disrespect. Pointing out that you have been disrespected is pretty far from fighting words. It didn't have any kind of calming effect. That's for sure. He immediately jumps into my face. I am still on the bike, straddling it under the bright streetlights of the Sunset Strip on that warm summer night. He fired back the following, laced with flawless logic.

"Oh, yeah, I don't think I disrespected you-but if you think I did we got a problem and we gonna have to do something about that." The kids are kind of dressed like corny out-of towners. Lotta Mervyns goin on, making me sense like San Bernardino or something… the kid is acting like a real douchebag, but not exactly an LA douchebag. It seems like he got his act from watching Yo MTV Raps too many times, not from the real streets. [When I found that a high percentage of kids that had played Grand Theft Auto had been in a lot of street fights, it didn't surprise me in the least]

"What?!" Now my little internal anger dial has gone up from about four to 45,000. But I stay cool. I think I have that quality that some exceptionally violent people have. If I am angry, I will yell and scream. If I am getting ready to get crazy, I become silent and outwardly calm. Like an alligator that is sneaking up on you. This kid is not making sense, he's a dick and he's in my face. He's also ENORMOUS.

"I didn't ask you to fight, I said the way you treated me was disrespectful."

"Yeah, well you gotta shake my hand now or we gonna have to settle this another way." He sticks out his hand.

I reluctantly shake his fucking hand that is the size of a catcher's mitt.

"OK, man, now you got to shake the spot." Which means he wants me to leave. He learned this one from watching something with Ice Cube in it. His earlier work, not the movies where Ice Cube acts like he's the black Clark W. Griswold.

"No, dude, I'm going to chill here for a minute, you can go anywhere you want.' **Anger dial is now melted.**

"Look, you gots ta get the fuck ON!" What was this guy, the fire marshall, mayor of my personal space?

I'm still on the bike and I kind of shake my head and his buddies pull him away. Antagonizing a stranger aside, his act really smells and must have been embarrassing. Go back and study some more raps songs, take a Menacing Black Guy class at the local Learning Annex or something. Beginner Level.

They walk about thirty feet down the block and I turn to go away, angered, humiliated and trippin balls when his buddy comes over and tells me he's sorry for his friend's conduct. My anger is like a howling wind inside me.

Not really wanting to hear this, I tell him that what his friends do reflect on him, or some other asinine old white guy Mr. Rogers shit, and he walks back… and must have reported what I said because the big black kid starts yelling "WHAT THE FUCK DID YOU JUST SAY? WHAT THE FUCK?" And comes running at me.

That's not good.

I am on my bike; I can just roll it down the steep hill to Fountain Avenue and escape. I have plenty of time to do this. Eighty percent of me wanted to split.

Nah.

I get off my bike, and put down the kickstand and stand with my arms at my sides as he comes right up to me screaming in my face and, as he makes the last step I time the hardest punch I have ever thrown. It's a beauty.

It's a right hook with a short radius with every ounce of my 200 pounds in it. He's tall, and so it's kind of like swinging an axe at a tree. There's a little extra on it because I am terrified, pissed and pretty damn insecure about being able to finish. I also have these Popeye forearms from swinging a hammer for ten years. It just blasts him right below his left ear and he drops to his knees like a trapdoor opened underneath him. He looks up at me dumbly and I put another one of the same on his cheekbone. I am working quickly but not hurrying. I am not going to miss or lose my balance from panic or anger. Miss? The kid's head is the size of a microwave oven. I drop about eight or ten more of these perfect bombs into the center of his face, any one of these punches would have broken a normal person's orbitals, as the mighty giant is *still*

188

trying to struggle to his feet to kill me. Each one lands with a scary thud. Blood starts spraying everywhere. I get it all over my green pants. This is pretty unusual for a fistfight, but this was a **real** horror show. I can't possibly relate the damage being done. His face is starting to look like a rotten pumpkin that someone has kicked in and the swelling hasn't even begun yet.

His buddies are stunned but then jump into action, tackling me onto the street and I am on my back trying to kick them off while cars whiz by. Somehow I get them off me, yelling at them that he started it. The huge black kid is trying to fight an imaginary enemy he can't see a few feet behind them. He is blinded and his face is disfigured. I jump on my bike and whiz down the hill laughing like I have never laughed.

At Santa Monica Boulevard and Vista, I am still laughing and I pull into an Astro Burger. The former Death Row Records mogul, and first ballot Hall of Famer Tough Guy, Suge Knight is there getting out of an enormous Escalade, I say "Hey Suge!" He smiles and looks at me and I tell him he needs to update his image and get a hybrid. Yes, I told Suge Knight to get a hybrid. That really happened.

In the middle of the night, I wake up in a panic, I have killed him, I think, I pray his friends had the sense to take him straight to the hospital. Time passes. The police don't show up. His death is not in the news. The big dummy lived apparently.

That particular fight is maybe the only one I felt really got out of control, that there was way too much damage; I hurt someone far too badly. I am sad.

I know that he was just trying to impress his friends; he was probably insecure… probably, well, a bunch of things.

Maybe next time he'll find a licensed social worker to act stupid, disrespectful, threatening and violent with.

189

CHAPTER THIRTY:
AFTERWARD

Anne, my younger sister and my friend Selima suggested the topic of this book. I thought that they were joking, maybe they were. Because I am not a member of The Aryan Brotherhood, The Hells Angels, Fight Club, and am not 14 years old, the topic of my fighting has mostly been an embarrassment. I really don't know anyone who has had half as many fights as I have had. There were times I didn't punch someone out who richly deserved it because there was like a little timer in my head telling me my last fight had been too recent. There were guys I didn't punch out because they were too weak, small or drunk.

I have gotten many opinions on the topic of this book. One old girlfriend was disappointed that I would want to re-live and revel in all of these brawls. Another girl remarked that at least I fought for a reason, where the guys that fought on TV were fighting pointlessly. I liked her take, which is the opposite of common sense, because those guys **are getting paid,** which I pointed out to her.

I know that I have purposefully not been invited to parties, for fear that I would punch someone out. "That Pat… too much of a wild card." Not that I necessarily start fights. They fear one of their other guest will start a fight with me and I will turn a wedding reception into the Me Lai massacre [that would never happen.] I have had friends say that they are hesitant to go out with me because often the night will end in some stupid brawl. One of those friends is named William.

William is an aspiring actor and an aspiring MMA fighter who is 6'5" tall. When we went to a Super Bowl party three weeks ago, he warned me not to get into any trouble. I said that was the furthest thing from my mind. Some of the guests were indeed rude, but I kept a smile on my face and made friends, as usual. William and I went out to a bar called St. Nicks in Hollywood just this past Friday night. It must have been Dickbag-palooza. Bring in an obnoxious asshole and drink for free. William was rudely shoved by a guy who made a real smartass apology. He then went over to his friends and spent 20 minutes mocking William. In my opinion, William is too nice of a guy. He never gets mad. He said that he had to leave, or else he was going to choke the guy silly. I laughed and asked "Which guy?" but William wisely refused to tell me. I told him that I would join him as soon as I finished my beer.

As I am finishing my beer, a very attractive and very drunk girl makes a beeline for me and begins chatting me up. Another guy rudely interrupts us and drags her away, almost forcibly. I sigh. I get up and go to the restroom. Some douchecake walks in as I am unzipping my pants and says, "HEY WHATS UP ASSHOLE?" I looked at him and he says, "HEY JUST KIDDIN BRO, LOTSA ACTION OUT THERE, YOU GONNA GET SOME, GET AFTER IT BRO?"

I looked at him, zipped up my pants and walked out of the bathroom without taking a leak. I went back to the bar and got as far away as possible from where that guy was sitting and waited for him to come and bother me some more. I was planning to crack his head on the sidewalk just on GP. It's been about two years since I had a fight, he could have grabbed that "Luckiest 100th Customer Slot." He never came.

I told William about it, assuming it was the same guy. It wasn't. There were at least two guys in there that were going around bothering two fairly dangerous individuals for… *I can never figure out what*.

I have been in 35-40 fights. In a world of perfect bar room justice, it should have been 135 [with *me* getting punched out 10 times], and it could have been 235.

I met two really cool exchange students, medical students, from A Dangerous Middle Eastern Country. They were excited to go to Guitar Center to jam on guitars.

In their country, a very small minority of Muslim Fascists, *won't let anyone* play electric guitar, even in the privacy of their own home.

If they are in the minority, then how are they forcing their retarded will on everyone else? [That curiosity is a recurring them in some Mid East countries.] It's because they are bullies and nobody wants to pay the price to stand up to them.

Today I walked up to the Coffee Bean, the kid, lets call him Norman Failure, is sitting solo at the table-for-six again. I put my stuff down and just moved his shit out of the way. I gave him the pleasant half-smile and thousand-mile stare I reserve for Special Occasions.

He sulked mightily for five minutes while I hoped he was going to say something. He petulantly moved his punk ass to another table. I was kind of disappointed he didn't say anything because the "sharing the table cheerfully rule" is right there on the Coffee Bean Wi-Fi page, right after they tell you to "please enjoy a beverage so we can keep providing free internet." *I* always cheerfully share the big table like Mr. Rogers riding the damn Welcome Wagon of Love. I like being polite and sharing.

You gotta try be nice, folks. At least at first. But you don't have to be nice forever, especially when you figure out you are no longer dealing with nice people.

Don't be bullied on your own accord. How do you deal with a bully? Mama Bettis? PUNCH HIM IN THE MOUTH.

WRITING ABOUT FIGHTING

I had some fun retelling these stories, but man, am I BURNT OUT on the whole fight subject. I never really wrote about them before and probably will never write about them again. Here is a better example of the type of non-violent musings I am more fond of having:

This weekend I went down to Venice Beach, to play a little hoop and ref a semi-pro basketball tournament. I am the worst referee ever. Because I play the game roughly, I just never called any fouls. Everyone was screaming at me. I'm probably the only ref in the history of the sport who did not call one foul the entire game. I had the whistle in my mouth, I just never blew into it… that's another story.

I was late getting back to the game after halftime, but I passed maybe the coolest thing I ever saw. Unfortunately, I had no time to stop to watch. Bummer.

Two very bold fifteen year-old girls decided to get in on the Venice street-performing gig. They wore matching baseball shirts and jeans shorts. They both had long hair in pigtails. They also had makeup on which would indicate that they were cats. Circle on the nose, six magic marker whiskers... um, that was about it. Zero effort on the costume front.

They made cat noises (pretty good ones) and acted like cats, meowing and hissing at each other. They clearly had the greatest gift that God ever gave a human: They clearly didn't give a fuck.

Nobody stopped to watch them.

The country that invented rock and roll, the airplane, electricity and the phone, has also brought you these two. You shall not find their counterpart in Sweden, Germany, Romania, China or Dubai.

God, I LOVE this country.

Acknowledgements:

I'D LIKE TO THANK GOD FOR THIS LIFE!

And the following humans:

My sister Anne, who really was the wind beneath my fists for this book, with constant praise and encouragement, a great sister, friend and book editor. If you think there too many enough of those … dot dot dot, things, don't blame her she made me take out about… fifty of them...

My friend and editor, Rick Redlich, wow, he did a great job at cleaning up sentences and adding jokes. Rick calls me "Shark-Man" because my violence and sexual appetites and "Joe 37-fitty," kind of a take-off on Joe Millionaire, because I carry my life-savings on my person at all times and it usually amounts to about $37.50.

Lanai Winter, longtime friend and amazing supporter.

My dad whose honesty and hard work enabled me to eventually become… I don't know, something I am proud of. Thanks for all the food, education, books, toys, clothes, shelter and above all, Glen Ayre membership. Fare the well, my ramblin boy. Rest in peace.

My mom whose toughness is hilarious and hilariousness is legendary. She has bailed me out of the two worst financial scrapes and many others. She is just great.

My first boxing instructor. Bob Beals may be partially responsible for some of the mayhem detailed in this book.

My excellent teachers throughout the years: Mrs. D, Mrs. Fagan, Shawn Shifflett, Al Coppersmith, Miss Dill, Mrs. Egan, Ron Hible and others!

Will Swaim who gave me my first writing gig.

And the countless friends who helped me through my countless tough times: Wayne Benson, Kevin O'Shea, Lois and Al Benson [who rescued me from being a street person], German Bravo, Chip Dempsey, my mom, Rick Redlich, Max Kucher. Wayne Dottenwhy, Phil Levine, Sandy Wolfson, Jim Comiskey [who once gave me a Hyundai I failed to register and was besieged by the DMV…best line ever: Did you kill anyone in the car yet, Patrick?]

Thank you all so much… God Bless

I will close with one of my favorite proverbs:

"No need to give too much to a man, with a jug of wine and a loaf of bread I have often won me a friend."